TRIBUTE

TRIBUTE

☆ ☆ ☆

Honoring America's Warriors

The Military Book Club
New York

About our background notes: We've included some brief, broad-stroked sketches to help coming generations understand the context that the people on these pages lived through. They offer some insights and additional information and are by no means complete. Just as no history of American fighting men and women can be complete.

Book design by Shonna Dowers

Printed in U.S.A.

FOREWORD

The Military Book Club® has been privileged to serve veterans and the military community for over thirty years. *Tribute* is our way of honoring and celebrating those people.

We knew that many of our members have long wanted to share memories of their own service and record their remembrances of husbands, fathers, brothers, and buddies who gave part—and some the ultimate part—of their lives for our nation. This permanent record . . . this connection between the generations is, we hope, the start of a tradition at The Military Book Club® and a fitting testimonial.

Honor, fortitude, sacrifice, humor in the face of adversity, loyalty, brotherhood and, too frequently, the "last full measure of devotion," are all to be found within the pages of this book. They are eternal values and we are proud to record them for posterity.

—Michael Stephenson
Editor-in-Chief
TRIBUTE

CONTENTS

☆ ☆ ☆

CIVIL WAR DIARY OF
HENRY W. TISDALE
by Mark F. Farrell/great-grandson

HENRY W. TISDALE, post Civil War

Henry W. Tisdale was born on March 9, 1837, in Walpole, Massachusetts, the eldest of seven children. He grew up in Walpole and West Dedham, which today is Westwood, Massachusetts. On July 10, 1862, at the age of twenty-five, he enlisted in the Union Army, Company I, Thirty-fifth Regiment, Massachusetts Volunteers, and was given the rank of sergeant. Henry was the first from Dedham to enlist when President Lincoln issued his call for 300,000 volunteers. The regiment trained at Camp Stanton in Lynnfield, Massachusetts. Henry was employed as a clerk at Mr. Bogden's market at the time of his enlistment.

Shortly after enlisting Henry was wounded in the thigh

by a minie ball at South Mountain, Maryland, on September 14, 1862. This kept him away from the regiment until February 4, 1863, when it left for Kentucky and East Tennessee. Later in 1863, Henry participated in the Vicksburg and Jackson, Mississippi campaigns.

On July 13th, while at Jackson, Henry was giving instructions to a sergeant of the Seventh R.I., when a minie ball struck the sergeant, killing him instantly. It then passed through him and struck the middle band of Henry's rifle, saving Henry's life. The rifle was dented and splintered and now held special meaning. The regiment spent the next few months in East Tennessee.

During 1864, the Thirty-fifth Regiment participated in Grant's campaign in Virginia. On May 24th, Henry was captured during an attack following the North Anna River crossing where he was forced to give up his battle-scarred rifle. He was sent to several prisons, including: Libby Prison in Richmond; Andersonville in Georgia (from June 7 until October 9, 1864); and Camp Lawton in Millen, Georgia. While at Andersonville Henry was the sergeant of Detachment seventy-six and was responsible for ninety fellow prisoners. His duties included obtaining rations for the sick of the detachment and getting them to the prison hospital. Henry was finally exchanged on March 3, 1865, and was discharged from service on June 13th after three long years of war.

On June 3, 1868, he married Abigail F. Cheney and they had seven children. About 1870 the family moved to West Roxbury, Massachusetts, where Henry opened a grocery store and market. Henry was a deeply religious man throughout his life and never talked about his Civil War exploits with his family. Henry died on May 31, 1922, at the age of eighty-five and was buried in Highland Cemetery in Norwood, Massachusetts.

☆ ☆ ☆ October 29, 1862 ☆ ☆ ☆
South Mountain, Maryland

Some six weeks have passed away since writing. They have been eventful ones to me, full of God's providential goodness and mercy. A good deal of the time have been unable to write, and the remaining time have been indisposed to it. At near 4 P.M. September 14th, our Brig. was ordered to the front; a rough march of some four miles brought us to the scene of conflict, climbing steep hills, some almost mountains, crossing rough fields, thru corn fields, and some of the way at double quick. On our way meeting many wounded being carried to the rear and as we neared the battle ground, here and there a dead body was to be seen. At little after 5 P.M. were upon the ground where the booming of artillery told us we were mid the stern realities of actual battle. The sight of the wounded sent a kind of chill over me, but in the main, feelings of curiosity and wonder at the scenes about me, took hold of my mind. Were drawn up in line of battle in a cornfield, and then advanced thru a sort of wooded field to a thick wood, where we met the rebels or a few scattering ones for their main body was now on the retreat. In entering the wood came upon a large number of rebel dead lying in a ravine, presenting a sad and sickening sight. They were making an advance upon our lines, but when crossing the ravine were met by a volley from the 17th Mich., which so thinned their ranks that on that part of their line they made a precipitate retreat. Just after we entered the wood was wounded by a rifle ball passing thru my left leg just opposite the thigh bone. As the ball struck me it gave me a shock, which led me to feel at first that the bone must have been struck and shattered, and for a moment did not dare to move for fear it was so. Found on moving that the bone was not injured and that I had only a flesh wound, which relieved my mind, and thankfulness to God that I was not maimed or dangerously hurt came. Think that the shot must have been fired by some straggling rebel or sharp shooter in a tree, as we had not yet got up to within reach of the rebel lines. Found myself in a few moments growing weak and tying my towel above the wound to stop its bleeding tried to make for the rear where the surgeons were. As I was limping off, a wounded rebel who was sitting against a tree called me and asked if I did not have something to eat; exhibiting a loaf and going to him, I opened my knife to cut off a slice, when he placed his hands before his face exclaiming "don't kill me," begging me to put up the knife and not to hurt him. Assuring him I had no intention of hurting him, I spoke with him a little. Found he had a family in Georgia, that he was badly wounded and was anxious to have me remain with him and help him off. But found that I was growing weaker from loss of blood and that the surging to and fro of the troops about us, made it a dangerous place, so limping and crawling was obliged to leave him and move to the rear. Soon came across some men detailed to look out for the wounded, who placed me in a blanket and took me to the rear to the surgeon. The place where the wounded were brought was near a cottage near which had been the battle ground of the forenoon. Was fortunate enough to be placed upon a straw bed in the garden just outside the house and had my wound promptly dressed. The cottage had a memento of the fight in the shape of a hole thru the roof made by a cannonball. The fighting continued til late in the evening. Our Regt losing but a few wounded, among them our Col. lost his left arm, and Geo. E. Whiting of our Co., one of his feet. He bore the amputation manfully. The house, outbuildings and the ground adjoining them were filled and covered with wounded, rebel and union mingled, all being cared for as best they could be; many moaning piteously throughout the night or til death put an end to their sufferings. Friend S. R. Baker of our Co. took care of us of the Regt., doing what he could and adding much to our comfort amid the confusion and suffering existing about. On the afternoon of Tuesday, September 16th, a train of ambulances came and all of us able to be moved were taken to Middlestown and placed in the churches, vacant buildings, etc. in the town. Endeavored to get into the same building with Whiting, but in vain. Was saddened to hear of his death while at Frederick City, from dysentary and weakness from his wound. Remained at Middletown until the next afternoon; the citizens generously supplying us with food and other needs; when we were moved to Frederick City, and were place in the Lutheran Church which was turned into a hospital. A rough board floor was laid over the tops of the pews. Folding iron bedsteads with mattresses, clean white sheets, pillows, blankets, clean underclothing, hospital dressing gowns, slippers, etc. were furnished us freely. The citizens came in twice a day with a host of luxuries, cordials, etc. for our comfort. The church finely finished off within, well ventilated and our situation as pleasant and comfortable as could be made. A few rebel wounded were in the building. Some of the citizens showed them special attention, bringing them articles of food etc., and giving none to the others. The surgeon put a stop to this, however, by telling them that they must distribute to all alike or they would not be allowed to visit the hospital at all—this was much to our satisfaction.

☆ ☆ ☆ July 13, 1863 ☆ ☆ ☆
Near Jackson, Mississippi

Were divided, four men to a post during the night, two required to be on the watch at a time—thus got four hours sleep during the night. Just as day broke the rebs opened fire quite savagely; at the same time we were relieved by the 7th R.I. Many of this Regt. were wounded, a few killed in getting their position. Had a very narrow escape—viz. I was standing behind an orderly, Sergt of the 7th, who had relieved me—both of us behind a tree, I giving him some instructions. I had my gun in front of me lengthwise of my body— felt a click upon my gun and at the same moment the Sergt uttered a faint cry and fell upon his face at my feet. I sprang close to the tree and glancing at the body saw the blood gushing from his mouth and that a bullet had passed thru his body. He uttered a groan and expired. Looking at my gun I saw that the middle band was partially broken and the woodwork close to it dented upon the barrel, thus showing that the bullet after passing thru his body had struck the gun and by it was glanced aside. Thus again has God preserved me in the day of battle. How strange the fortunes of war. All the day before I had been at the same spot and not always careful to keep behind the tree—thoughtless of real danger. In fact not five minutes before the Sergt. was killed, I spread out my blanket in an open spot near the tree and folded it and yet not a shot was fired at me. Dropping upon my knees I crawled quickly to the rear and was soon out of danger once more. Felt sober the rest of the day. Feel that while God is thus, almost by direct providence, shielding my life I ought to render it all as an offering of gratitude to His service. Our Regt. remained in support of the skirmish line the rest of the day. Were ordered to keep equipment on and ready to fall in line of battle at a moment's notice. Twice we were thus ordered to fall in but proved only a feeble attempt of the "rebs" to drive our skirmish line, which caused the order. It was amusing to see us scrabling to get into line as these orders came. Some would be cooking coffee, which of course would have to be dumped instantly; some semi-asleep. Visited the camp of the 7th R.I. and ascertained that the man shot before me was unmarried and was much esteemed in the regiment.

☆ ☆ ☆ May 23, 1864 ☆ ☆ ☆
Virginia

March at 6 P.M. A good road most of the way. Very dusty, one slough hole kept us hitching along for near 3 hours, going meanwhile but 2 miles, after this a race to catch up. Our regiment acting as provost guard, our duty to look out for and catch all stragglers and send them to their regiments. Think our commanding officer showed lack of feeling towards many of them who were really exhausted and part sick. They were treated roughly and with needless severity. The job of picking up stragglers in times of rapid marching on these hot days, is not a pleasant one, it being often hard to tell who are "playing off" and who really is tired and foot sore. Think some of our surgeons are not particular enough and willing enough to give permits, that the latter class may have their knapsacks and accourterments put upon the teams. Halted and made coffee at 3 P.M. Made some 12 miles and camped 1 miles from the No. Anna River at 7 P.M. Heavy cannonading in the distance near all the afternoon. Our route the past 2 days has been thru a fine farming country, with here and there a field of corn, wheat or tobacco, but most fields growing weeds and the farm buildings and houses deserted. In some, a few women or old negroes could be seen; many of them were badly frightened at our (the Yanks) coming. At one house the females, evidently young ladies, amused themselves and us by calling us names and screeching at us. One of the regiments cleared out one house, smashing the furniture and carrying off things of no use to them. Generals Grant and Meade, and staffs, passed us today. Well tired out as we stretched out for sleep in a rough cornfield, with a full moon over our heads.

☆ ☆ ☆ May 24th ☆ ☆ ☆

Slept soundly. Woke fully refreshed. Lounged about under orders to be ready to move at once, until 1 P.M., when were again on the march. It was warm and dusty. One mile brought us to the No. Anna River. This we forded, water hip deep, the bottom of the river rough and rocky, the current strong. Swung our haversacks (heavy with 3 days rations) and our cartridge boxes over our heads and shoulders. Some were unlucky enough to get upset and came near getting drowned. After crossing, our brigade was formed in battle line. Our regiment deployed as skirmishers and led the advance thru a thick, fine wood, ravines and rough places in plenty with here and there an open space, going some of the way at double quick time. We soon met the rebel picket line which fell back at our advance, saluting us at the first with a few stray buck shots. A half a mile or more brought us to an open field beyond which we could see the rebel breastworks, batteries and infantry in battle line. Halted until our brigade came up when a general attack was made upon the rebel line in our front with the result of driving them to their main line. Continuing the advance we were met with such a shower of shell, grape, and canister combined with a sudden downpour of rain, that our lines were broken and orders were given to fall back to the breastwork which our reserves had thrown up in our rear. In the scrimmage our regiment line was broken up as we fell back thru the woods. Suddenly found myself alone with 3 of our 35th and the main body of the 56th. Going up to Gen. Leddlie, I asked for the whereabouts of the 35th. He said they were all mixed up with the other regiments and I had better go in with the 56th. Joined them and tried to find some of the 35th, but in vain and soon concluded that the place for me was with my own regiment and started back to the river. Soon came upon Capt. Hudson and Co. H., who were doing picket duty on the left. He did not know where the rest of the regiment was. We remained in quiet for near an hour when a downpour of rain came on, in the midst of which the rebels succeeded in getting our flank, which caused a "grand skidadle" on our part toward the river. We stopped to give a wounded man some water. I got separated and found myself alone and mid the rain, mist and woods, began to be in doubt as to the line of retreat when I came upon Lt. Creasy and 2 other staff officers chatting unconcernedly, so felt all right and kept on coming out to an open field, when I came upon a line of skirmishers lying upon the ground. Marching towards them, supposing them our own men, when suddenly a half dozen or more jumped up, took aim and yelled "drop that gun"—kept on towards them yelling out "don't fire on your own men," only to receive a second yell from them. Then to suddenly realize that death or surrender was my alternative and with a feeling of shame and mortification, threw down my gun which I had hoped to carry home (with scar of rebel bullet received at Jackson, Mississippi) as a memorandum of the war. Was soon taken in charge by a member of the 7th Alabama with a reproof for not dropping my gun at their first call, and the remark that "in another minute you would have been a dead man." Marched to the rear, was relieved of rubber blanket, shelter tent and cartridge box, and found myself with about 25 more unfortunates. Was humiliated to find myself alone of the 35th at first, but not for long for soon came in the 3 staff officers and 5 comrades of the 35th. Were marched about a mile to Anderson's Station, where we found more of the wearers of the blue and by night we numbered about 70. Our guards treated us well. As we stretched out upon Mother Earth, another shower greeted us, so that with our previous duckings, we were so well soaked that our weary bodies soon forgot it all in "nature's sweet restorer, balmy sleep."

☆ ☆ ☆ May 25th ☆ ☆ ☆

Slept soundly. Fine morning and with the opening day 3 more of the 35th were brought in, making 9 of us. As the day grew, it became warmer and we were taken into a wood where it was cool and comfortable. The rebel soldiers were anxious to buy watches, knives, paper and jewelry, paying in Confederate money now worth in exchange value 1/10th of United States money. They were in the main good solid looking men, well clothed many having on some part of U.S. uniforms. Those wearing our army belts did so with the U.S. upside down. Were free to talk with us. At near 3 P.M. shot from some distant batteries began to roll in among us and soon we were in a grand "skidaddle" to the rear for about a mile. At 4 P.M. came the words "fall in, forward march" and a march of 5 miles brought us to Taylorsville where we halted, to then start a 10 mile march to Ashland where we were permitted to camp on a fine grassy plot. During the march in the P.M. passed several regiments of confederates evidently waiting orders and lining the roadsides. Got a good ducking on the way. Missed Uncle Sam's rubber blankets. While halted for a rest saw a young confederate whose face looked familiar but could not recall his name or where I had seen him before. He recognized me and found him to be Charles Ellis, whose father, a former Mass. man, had removed to Florida and at the opening of the war had espoused the cause of the confederacy. He, with his brother Frank, were schoolmates of brothers Ronnie and Herbert. Charles was in the 2nd Florida and Frank in a regiment of Texas Rangers. Was quite affected to see me, inquiring minutely about his former schoolmates and relations still living in his former Northern home; to be sure and tell his relatives of my seeing him should I live to get home.

☆ ☆ ☆ June 3rd ☆ ☆ ☆

A heavy shower at near 11 o'clock last night. It gave us a good out-side bath and reminded us that we were without any of the U.S. goodly tents. The day opened warm as luck would be, and we soon dried off. On the cars again—box cars, 65 to a car, so crowd-ed we could scarce move and the air not very pure. Fortunately a good many of us were allowed to ride on tip of the cars. One hun-dred eight miles and at near dark were at Columbia, So. Carolina. The aspect of the country along the route, not so thrifty as in No. Carolina. Corn and wheat seemed to be nearly all the crops in growth, with here and there a vegetable patch. Saw but one field of cotton. Changed cars for Augusta, Georgia. Had better accom-modations as we were not so crowded.

☆ ☆ ☆ June 6th and 7th ☆ ☆ ☆

Slept uncomfortably on account of heat. Were allowed to fraternize with citizens who were willing to give us confederate money in exchange for our "greenbacks" if we were lucky enough to have any at the ratio of 10-1, and also to buy all the watches and jewelry we would sell. Pratt was the only one of our mess who had a watch. This he found he could sell for $100 (confederate). We felt a little money in our pocket would not come amiss, so the sale was made and we agreed to share alike in spending the money and in replac-ing the watch in the happier days we hoped in store for us, "When Johnny Comes Marching Home." Bought some cornbread to splice out our rations. At 2 P.M. were marched thru the city about 3/4 of a mile and were soon on the way to Andersonville, Georgia. Augusta as we saw it, seemed beautiful. The citizens treated us civilly and kindly, the boys willingly bringing us water. A ride of some 250 miles and at noon on Tuesday, June 7th, were landed on a grassy plot with "Andersonville Stockwall" in our front. Soon a wiry look-ing officer on a white horse rode along and gave orders to "fall in line." A squad of "blue jackets" for some reason, were not obeying orders, when the officer swore at them and ordered them into line.

This was our introduction to the prison cammondant, Captain Wirtz. He then displayed a sheet of letter paper and called for a Sergeant. It flashed upon me that this might mean some work to do and my dread of idle hours might be relieved, and I sprang forward, to be told to count off 90 men and enroll them upon the paper; that they made up the 3rd mess of detachment #76 and that my duties would be to have supervision over them. A daily roll call, a report, divide the rations and for this work was to have double rations. Just as the day closed we were marched thru the gates, many of us feeling that the words "Abandon hope all ye who enter here" might have a real meaning to us. Found it much worse place than I had expected or that it had been represented to us by the citizens while enroute. So crowded that it seemed as if there was no room for us newcomers to stretch out upon. Got a ducking and laid down for the night wet, but slept soundly. Another shower during the night.

☆ ☆ ☆ June 12th ☆ ☆ ☆

Five days rations, and is 5 days since writing; partly from want of time but more from want of disposition. For the first 3 days was busy getting my 90 reduced to order. Find much more work than I anticipated. Takes an hour and often more to get them together for roll call, get the names of the sick and those who are to go for wood. Another hour to go with sick and get medicines for them, another hour to get the wood squad together and go for wood and near 2 hours to divide the rations. The prison is one mess of human beings, crowded together, many without shelter from the sun and rain— those having shelters good enough to protect from rain are few. Most have made themselves shelters with wool blankets, overcoats, brush, twigs and dried mud; many have made caves and dugouts in the clayey soil. Thru the center runs a sluggish stream about 3 feet wide and bout half knee deep. On each side for about 2 rods in width is a sort of swamp hole which in wet weather is a fuse. It is never cleaned up and is a good deal of the time one seething mass of maggots. The stream is often full from before daylight until dark with bathers or others trying to wash their clothes in its muddy fluid. The camp includes some 15 acres inclusive of the swamp. Is surrounded by a stockade made of fine pine logs about 20 feet high. In sentry booths at intervals are stationed sentinels overlooking the camp. Just outside is a battery of 6 guns so placed as to overlook the prison. There is a hospital outside, but those who have seen it say it scarce deserves the name of hospital. Find that many have been here near a year. The upper part of the stream for about 12 or 15 feet is reserved for drinking water and most of the day its banks are crowded with water seekers. Nearby our camp spot a party of a dozen or more have been digging a well and have just come to drinking water, but how to get it was a problem to them as none of them had any kind of pail. Fortunately one of us four had a 3 pint tin pail to which a rope made of pieces of string and sundry old rags was soon tied. For the use of same we four were added to the gang of well diggers and had the privilege with them of free use of the well. About 15 feet from the stockade was the "dead line" made of 3 or 4 joists placed upon posts made of the same, standing about 3 feet high. This we were not allowed to touch, and quite often the sharp call of the sentinel "hands off," or occasionally the crack of the rifle and whiz of a bullet would greet the disobedient "Yanks." Was told there was a rebel sutler on the other side of the prison and soon ten dollars of our hoarded hundred was exchanged for a bar of soap about 12 inches by 1 1/2 inches square. A sad thing had happened the other day. Going down to bathe Pratt left his clothes on the bank and on resuming them he found that his pocketbook and our $90 was gone. He sat upon the bank and cried like a child saying "I don't care about the money if they had only left me the picture of my wife and child." This was our first introduction to a class of prisoners termed "Raiders." Talking over the matter with one of the older prisoners, he said there was a regular organized band of them who made it a business to rob and plunder each new arrival. Find the north side of the prison to be honeycombed with burrows and dugouts, some of them large enough to contain 20 men. Going over the prison and coming in contact with its inmates, one's eyes fill with tears and the heart shrinks in horror at the scenes around him— men most skeletons from lack of food, from diarrhea, chills and fever. Others are racked with rheumatism or bloated with scurvy; more than half clothed in rags. The rations are brought in the afternoon, meal and rice in 50 pound sacks. Cornbread in sheets about 18 by 24 inches and 2 or 3 inches thick, sometimes half cooked or cooked so hard as to endanger our teeth. Bacon sides form our meat rations, and no vegetables so that scurvy runs riot among the older prisoners. Some of my 90 already on the sick list. Yesterday went with 2 of them to sick call. The gathering place was between the two stockades, with 2 or 3 surgeons in attendance. Near 2,000 reported sick. It was the most heart-rending sight I ever saw. Men brought in blankets by scores weak and wan from diarrhea or bloated and loathsome from scurvy or scarce able to hobble from rheumatism. They begged to be sent to the hospital or that some kind of shelter might be given them from the sun or rain. Have drawn raw rations of corn meal and bacon the past 4 days. When raw rations are given out, 6 men from each 90 are allowed to go out, under guard, for wood. Have to go some half a mile and lug it in on our backs, thus 1 man has to lug enough for 15. Have managed to lug in some pine boughs to carpet our tent which is made of 2 wool blankets with 1 overcoat for our bed covering. The weather hot with a shower in the afternoon so far each day. Have felt dull and stupid today, think it is from the heat and change of food. Scarce any change from our week day routine of prison life. Came across my old townsman and christian brother today. He has been a prisoner 7 months. D. F. Nichols of the 18th Mass. Regiment. Six men sick with diarrhea today in my vicinity.

☆ ☆ ☆ June 13th ☆ ☆ ☆

Rain most of the night. Cold and drizzly all day. Hundreds of poor fellows soaked from last night's shower, are shivering about the camp. God pity and help them for none of us can do anything for them. Have reports that a portion of us are to be paroled soon.

☆ ☆ ☆ June 15th ☆ ☆ ☆

Today the third of a cold drizzly rain. It has made sad havoc with the poor fellows who have no shelter. We four have taken down our blankets the past two nights to keep warm, preferring wetting to freezing. Further acquaintance with the prison and its inmates, makes it more sad and sickening. The sick miserably cared for. The commanding officials show no sense of humanity, seem to have little executive ability to keep the camp clean and orderly. Prisoners are constantly trying to escape when let out for wood, etc. Seven escaped from the bakery yesterday and night before at least 18 tumbled out under the stockade. Not one in a hundred get to the land of liberty . . .

WILDERNESS CAMPAIGN OF 1864

The war was going badly for the Confederacy. By mid-1963, the Confederacy had effectively been beaten in the west. While the simultaneous defeat at Vicksburg and Gettysburg was a bitter rebuff to Confederate strategy, no effective exploitation was carried out by the Union. This prompted President Lincoln to promote the architect of victory in the west, General Grant, to commander of the entire Union army. Grant moved east and established his command with the Army of the Potomac (AoP), under General George Meade. Grant ordered an offensive on every front.

In 1864, the AoP began to move south into some of the most rugged and forbidding terrain in the nation. This region of Virginia is aptly called the Wilderness. Even in the mid-nineteenth century, it was sparely settled. Two Union armies had already been turned back with heavy losses when they tried to penetrate the Wilderness. General Robert E. Lee and the veteran Army of Northern Virginia (ANV) were confident they could turn back Grant as well.

They were wrong. Grant's original plan was to avoid battle and push through the Wilderness as quickly as possible. When contact with Lee began, he changed his plans and the battle that resulted was a bloodbath for both sides. While the Union troops suffered terrible losses, so did the ANV. General James Longstreet, Lee's "Old War Horse" was wounded and carried off the field.

When the smoke cleared, Lee expected to see the mauled AoP withdraw. Instead, Grant ordered an advance deeper into Virginia. Lee was off balance and had to race his battered forces south to counter Grant. It was a race he could not win.

Ultimately, Lee was forced to withdraw to the capitol of the Confederacy at Richmond and face the siege that would end the war.

MY GOD, THE JAPS ARE HERE

by Milton J. Elliott III

O n Sunday morning, December 7, 1941, Japan began its war against the United States with a devastating surprise attack on the U.S. Pacific Fleet at Pearl Harbor and on surrounding military installations in the Hawaiian Islands.

In about two hours, the Japanese sank or seriously damaged 18 warships, destroyed 188 aircraft, and damaged 159 more. The United States suffered 2,430 killed and 1,178 wounded. The Japanese lost 29 planes, 5 midget submarines, and 68 pilots and sailors.

Pearl Harbor, when the damage was compared to the losses sustained, was the least costly and most shattering victory in military history. William A. Rolfe of Richmond, Virginia, saw it unfold; he was there.

As America slumbered through 1940, at least one of its sons— Rolfe—yearned for more excitement than Richmond offered. He enlisted in the Army Air Corps in June and by August had been assigned to the Fifth Bomb Group at Hickam Field, a scant mile or so from Pearl Harbor where the U.S. Pacific Fleet, one of the world's most powerful naval forces, was based.

Until that morning at Pearl Harbor, the war spreading across Europe and Japanese aggression in the Far East barely had touched the lives of U.S. servicemen in the Pacific. Rolfe recalled the "lush mountains, blue tropical sea, fantastic beaches" of Hawaii. On weekends, ships and bases were manned by skeleton forces. It was, in a word or two, dream duty.

But that morning duty at Hickam Field became a nightmare.

The Japanese task force steaming toward the Hawaiian Islands received this intelligence report: No balloons, no torpedo-defense nets deployed around battleships in Pearl Harbor. All battleships in. No indications from enemy radio activity that ocean-patrol flights (are) being made.

"It was about eight o'clock," Rolfe recalled. "And I was dressing to go to church. I was sitting on the side of my bunk (in the barracks at Hickam Field) when I heard a rumbling noise outside. I rushed to the window and the first thing I saw was a plane headed toward me. It was a Japanese Zero and it buzzed about ten or fifteen feet over my head.

"My God, the Japs are here," I yelled to others in the barracks. Their reply, almost in unison, was "shut up, go back to bed, you're crazy." It didn't take long for them to realize I was right.

"We rushed out on the field, which was being strafed by the Japanese. It was chaos, no organization. Some men were crying and praying, some were trying to restore order. Since I was a member of the antisabotage squad, I had a Springfield (standard issue rifle), ammo, and gas mask in my locker. Others broke into the ordnance shack and grabbed what weapons they could find. About the only things in there were .45s (automatic pistols) and very little ammunition.

"Meanwhile, others had gone to the flight line to fuel and load 500-pound bombs on the B-18s (twin-engine bombers). Then the Japanese bombs started to hit. Many of the planes went up in flames, a buddy of mine was killed by the concussion, an officer with both legs shot off was begging someone to kill him, some of the men were firing their pistols at the planes. I was shooting at them with my Springfield.

"To add to the confusion, a flight of B-17s began to arrive from the States. They had no guns on board and couldn't defend themselves. They all got down but many were destroyed.

"There was a lull in the attack, maybe thirty-five or forty minutes. Then more planes came and started dropping bombs down the hangar line. They also hit some more of our parked B-18s. In about two hours it was over.

"We loaded the wounded on trucks to go to the hospital. We also loaded the dead on trucks. Then we started to disperse what was left of our airplanes and start salvage work. The rest of the day is sort of fuzzy.

"But that night, because everyone thought the Japanese were going to invade, we dug a lot of foxholes. I really didn't think about a war starting. I don't even recall being scared, but later that day, since they were giving away cigarettes, I started with a Lucky Strike. I hated the Japanese and could hardly wait to get back at them."

DON'T EVER CALL ME CHICKEN

By Richard A. Beranty

A veteran of the D-Day assault on Normandy and a defender
of Bastogne during the Battle of the Bulge, Ludwig J. "Lud" Labutka
of Ford City, PA, poses for the cameraman. Prominent in the
photo are the paratrooper's prized jump boots.

I n an effort to calm his nerves just before he jumped into
Normandy on D-Day, Lud Labutka thought it might be a good
idea to accept the drink he was being offered from the paratrooper
sitting across from him on their C-47 transport as it crossed the
English Channel. It didn't matter whether it came from a bottle of
bonded Scotch or from a bottle of after-shave lotion. Labutka was
simply looking for a little kick to help him get over the anxiety he

felt about jumping into Nazi-occupied Europe.

"There was this guy on our plane named Tom Jones," Labutka says. "He looked over at me and said, 'Lud, do you want a drink?' I said, 'What?' He said, 'Do you want a drink?' I still didn't think he had anything to drink until he pulled out a big bottle of Aqua Velva. I said, 'You're crazy!' He opened it and sucked down a drink. I said to him, 'Jones, if you're crazy, I'm crazy too.' This was 20 minutes before we jumped! So I took a big drink. When I jumped into Normandy, I was heaving. I was puking on the Germans. That stuff made me sick."

The idea of jumping from an airplane, or flying in one for that matter, had never occurred to seventeen-year-old Labutka when he joined the Pennsylvania National Guard in 1939. Even to this day his fear of heights has kept his feet planted to the ground.

"I wouldn't even go on the Ferris wheel at a fair," he says. "I still haven't been on one. I was afraid of heights."

If that's the case, then how does this seventy-nine-year-old from Ford City, Pennsylvania, explain his wartime experiences as a Screaming Eagle with the U.S. 101st Airborne Division, duty that took him not only into Normandy but also into Holland during Operation Market Garden? It's because someone, at some point, questioned whether he had the intestinal fortitude to jump from an airplane. In other words, it was the result of a dare.

"In 1942 the army was taking transfers into the Air Cadets," he says. "We were kids, just eighteen-, nineteen-, twenty-year-olds. Somebody mentioned airborne and I said, 'Airborne? Are you crazy? I'm not going to jump out of an airplane.' So somebody called me a chicken. That's all it took. I was going. We all figured that we'd make a difference, so three of us—Rich Dinger, Joe Miklos, and myself— went to see the first sergeant of our National Guard company and told him to transfer us to the airborne."

Labutka entered training on October 19, 1942, at Fort Benning, Georgia, where troops were hooked to guide wires and slid to the ground from forty-foot towers. "Scary" training, he admits. This progressed to actual jumps from an airplane, five of which were required to qualify for airborne duty.

"The first time I was up in an airplane I jumped. Back then we packed our own parachutes. At that time they were round, really huge things. Then, after jump school, riggers packed them. Every time I jumped I always wondered if the riggers had placed that little rubber band where it was supposed to be. It held the end of the parachute to the static line."

Labutka left Benning for Fort Bragg, North Carolina, the new home of the 101st where its men trained by making twenty-five-mile forced marches without water, running the last mile back to camp in cadence, and more practice jumps, often in front of such dignitaries as Gen. George C. Marshall, Army Chief-of-Staff. During this time he was assigned to the division's 502nd Parachute Infantry Regiment (referred to as the "Five-O-Two"), Second Battalion, E Company, First Platoon, and left for Europe in a convoy from Camp Shanks, New York, on September 5, 1943, aboard an aging British transport ship. It encountered engine trouble six days out, left the group and put in at the small Newfoundland harbor of St. John's where repairs were made. But as the ship headed to sea once again, it scraped bottom. Arrangements were then made for the troops to make the Atlantic crossing on the S.S. Ericsson which left port in another convoy and arrived at Liverpool on October 19th. It took Labutka forty-four days to reach England on a voyage usually made in a week.

"The convoy we joined contained Company C of my old National Guard outfit," he says. "By then they were the Twenty-eighth Division. I didn't know it at the time but I went overseas with my old buddies from Company C of the National Guard."

Once on British soil, men of the 502nd lived in tent cities at Denford Lodge near Hungerford where they made more practice jumps in preparation for their assigned role on D-Day. Since the division had no battle history up to that point and its men were an untested force, it seemed to other G.I.s in England that these so-called Screaming Eagles were a group of overpaid and overly cocky servicemen more famous for their fancy jump boots than for anything else. All of that changed, however, when they jumped from their C-47 transports in the pre-dawn darkness of Normandy, fulfilling what Gen. William C. Lee, the division's first commanding general, described as their "rendezvous with destiny."

Four objectives were assigned to the 101st in Operation Overlord. The paratroopers were first to secure the roadways leading from Utah Beach where the U.S. Fourth Division was to land. Second, eliminate a battery of large German guns which threatened that invasion beach. Third, establish contact with the Fourth

Division as it headed inland. And fourth, with those missions accomplished, attack and occupy the French town of Carentan, an important road junction leading to the Cotentin Peninsula and the port of Cherbourg. Labutka's Second Battalion was part of the force charged with eliminating the six-gun battery of 122 mm. howitzers at St. Martin de Varreville, two kilometers west of Utah Beach. Gen. Omar Bradley, U.S. ground commander, called the guns a danger to the invasion forces and insisted that they be eliminated.

Another anticipated danger, this one limited to airborne troops only, was the Normandy darkness and how paratroopers would know the difference between friend and foe. Brig. Gen. Maxwell D. Taylor, who assumed command of the 101st in March, solved this problem by introducing one of the most ingenious tools used in the invasion: the cricket. Basically a toy like those found in Cracker Jack boxes at the time, it proved extremely helpful for paratroopers to identify each other in the dark. The toy clicked when the tab on its back was pressed and released. One push asked, "Who's there?" Two pushes in reply meant, "Friend." A last-minute idea of Taylor's, the crickets arrived about four days before the invasion.

In late May the 101st was moved into new tent cities near the air-fields from which the men would fly to assault the German positions in France. On June 5th at about 5:30 P.M., the paratroopers ate their last pre-invasion meal of pork chops and mashed potatoes and returned to their assembly areas to reflect on what was in store for them and to take on their gear. It included an M-1 rifle with eight or ten clips, six grenades, two canteens, parachutes, flares, a medical kit, compass, and enough C-Rations for three days. All told, their equipment weighed about seventy pounds. As evening drew on, Labutka's platoon leader, 1st Lt. Wallace C. Stroebel, called his men away from their packing for some last minute instructions. As they gathered outside their tents, Gen. Dwight D. Eisenhower, Allied Supreme Commander, paid the men a visit. A photograph was taken of this encounter and it became one of the most famous of the pre-D-Day invasion. In it, Eisenhower is standing on the left talking to Stroebel. The two are shown in an apparent conversation about the invasion. When asked years later about what was said, Stroebel (who died in 1999) recalled that, in part, it went like this:

"Where are you from, lieutenant?" Eisenhower asked.

"Michigan, sir," replied Stroebel.

"Michigan, eh?" Eisenhower commented. "Good fishing in that country."

☆ ☆ ☆

Labutka, standing behind several men in the rear of the picture, says he never heard the conversation.

"We heard earlier that Ike might come by and wish us luck," he says. "But I have no idea what he said to Lieutenant Stroebel. I wasn't close enough."

The men entered their C-47s at around 9:00 P.M. through the aircraft's rear door which stayed open for the entire flight. They moved in single file with the first man headed to the front of the plane. The paratroopers took their seats located on both sides of the aircraft facing one another. Along the ceiling of the plane's compartment stretched the static lines to which their parachutes were hooked just prior to the jump. The pilots were told to fly in a V formation of three planes each at an altitude of 500 feet to avoid German radar detection over the English Channel. Once they crossed the coast of France, the planes climbed to 1,500 feet and then descended to 400 feet for the jump. Pilots were instructed not to veer from their assigned flight paths. The distance to their drop zone was 136 miles and it took about an hour to reach it.

"We knew that it was about 100 miles from where we were in England to where we were going. We were told to take out these guns. They didn't tell us why, just that we had to take them out."

Labutka says the flight was uneventful until they reached the French coast when German guns below opened up on them. Since he and others of Second Battalion were in some of the first planes of the assault, they reached France relatively unscathed.

"Once we got over Cherbourg you could see the enemy shooting at us," he says. "It looked like the tracer bullets were coming out of a barrel. We could hear them hitting the wings going 'knick, knick, knick.' I was scared." That's when Labutka took a healthy swallow of Aqua Velva.

With his stomach now churning, the C-47 neared its drop point and a red light flashed that told the paratroopers that their jump time was near. It was just after midnight when a sergeant yelled, "Stand up and hook up!" Moments later a green light flashed and Labutka says he was the sixth or seventh man to leave the plane.

"The sergeant hit the first guy on the ass and said, 'Go!' We were lined up tight, right against each other," he explains. "We were taught to count, 'One thousand, two thousand' when we jumped. If we got to the third count and the 'chute didn't open, we were to pull the reserve parachute. That one was on our belly. The only thing I remember thinking when I jumped was, 'I hope I land.'"

Labutka landed near the town of St. Côme-du-Mont, just west of Carentan and south of the guns his battalion was ordered to destroy.

"I landed in a farm courtyard, all brick and all fenced in, right beside a hay wagon," he says. "The machine gunner landed in one corner of the courtyard. His name was Dempsey, from Rome, Georgia. In the other corner was Golembeski, he was a Pollack from Pennsylvania. They both came over to me and asked, 'Lud, what are we going to do?' Here, both of them were Pfc.'s and I was just a private and they're asking me what to do! So I said to find a door so we could get out of this courtyard. The night was very dark. We found a door, or a gate, and went out and bumped into a guy here and a guy there until there were six of us. We walked around, snuck around, crawled around. We didn't meet anybody else. None of us fired a shot. Finally, when it was just getting light, about 5:30 P.M., we were walking around this hedgerow and saw a road.

"We crouched down because we heard people walking and talking," Labutka continues. "These guys with me said, 'Lud!' And I said, 'Shah!' I had my clicker and when the noise got near I went, 'click-click' with the cricket. Boy, the nicest sound that I ever heard came back: 'click-click, click-click.' So we jumped out on the road. I'd say there were about sixty people there including a lieutenant-colonel, a lieutenant, and a couple of sergeants, so we joined them."

Others in the drop, however, weren't so lucky, particularly those who came in after the first wave. As the surprised Germans grasped the scope of the situation, these later planes received heavy doses of antiaircraft fire. Some pilots took evasive action, broke formation and went off course. Paratroopers were scattered around the countryside. Many landed in swamps, rivers and flooded fields. Others found themselves stuck in trees or in the middle of mine fields. Some planes took direct hits and crash-landed or burst into flames before impact. Because of the ground fire and confusion, the drop zone resembled a rectangle of about twenty-five by fifteen miles. Scattered troops sought each other throughout the day and into the next.

The gun emplacements at Varreville did not pose a problem when Labutka saw them on June 6th. They had been destroyed by Allied bombings just prior to D-Day and were void of German troops. It was there where he met his battalion commander, Col. Steve Chappuis, whose drop put him close to the guns.

"I'm glad we had the Air Corps," he says. "They knocked out a bunch of German guns. When I saw Colonel Chappuis, he was sitting cross-legged on this cement curb. He said, 'Well, it looks like the Air Force took care of the guns.'"

With that threat neutralized, the gathered troops of Second Battalion moved toward the roads leading south from Utah Beach. Securing them was the primary responsibility of Lt. Col. Robert G. Cole's Third Battalion. By 1:00 P.M. on D-Day, Cole and his men had made contact with elements of the Fourth Division coming inland from the beach and the paratroopers found their numbers increasing. Throughout June 6th and 7th, those scattered in the drop linked up into larger fighting groups. They were augmented by glider landings of division artillery troops that had arrived earlier. The massed paratroopers set their sights to the south and the division's final objective, the town of Carentan.

"I don't think we really got together with any sizeable force until about a day and a half after we landed," Labutka says, estimating that they then numbered about two regiments strong. "None of us had gotten any sleep, unless we slept standing up. It's hard to believe, but we did sleep standing up."

Carentan was a high-priority target assigned to the 101st because its main highway and railroad connected Cherbourg to St. Lo and ultimately Paris. If American forces didn't take the town, it could be used as a corridor for a counterattack against Utah Beach. Army intelligence estimated the size of the German garrison there at a battalion. As it turned out the enemy was more plentiful and extremely stubborn. The division's route of attack was down a road that ran through flooded fields and swamps. Labutka says paratroopers called it "Purple Heart Lane" for obvious reasons. The 502nd's Third Battalion was assigned the lead.

"The first time I really heard gunfire was going toward Carentan. The Germans had machine guns pointed right down this road going into the town. There were four bridges we had to cross and swamps were on both sides of us. As we fought our way down the road we had to run this way, run that way, run this way, kind of zig-zag our way down it."

It was here where Labutka first experienced the devastating effects of German 88s. He also encountered two airborne buddies from home and both were wounded.

"Once we started down this road I met Joe Miklos," Labutka says. "He got hit from a bomb burst. There was shrapnel in his leg and he was going back. After we crossed the second bridge, who do I see but Rich Dinger with a patch on his shoulder. He was hit pretty bad. He said, 'Lud, don't go down there. It's hell down there.' I said, 'Dick, I have to. My company's going down there.' Dinger was eventually shipped home. Further down the road I came across this poor soldier who was hit right above his ear. I could see the matter leaking out. He tried to talk to me. He wanted morphine. I asked him if he'd had any but he couldn't answer. He was gone. He must have been from the 3rd Battalion, Dinger's outfit, because they went in ahead of us."

The German 88s were finally silenced but not before the road's second bridge was shattered to pieces. This kept supplies from being brought in and the wounded taken out. It also prevented a retreat by those on the road. Regardless, the paratroopers advanced, crossed the third bridge and ran into their stiffest resistance at the other side of the fourth bridge. It was a heavily-defended farmhouse about 150 yards away. With Col. Cole and men of Third Battalion still in the lead, intense fire from German machine guns, mortars and artillery pinned them to the ground for an hour. Knowing his men were low on ammunition, Cole ordered an attack with fixed bayonets and personally led the charge over open ground and eventually flushed the enemy from its positions. The charge established a bridgehead across the Douve River and earned Cole the Medal of Honor, the division's first awardee in Normandy. He never learned of it, however, as he was killed by a sniper's bullet in Holland just months later.

"That Major Cole was a soldier," Labutka offers. "I know Miklos didn't like him much because he was too hard on the men. But he was a soldier through and through."

While division engineers worked to make the second bridge passable, the badly depleted Third Battalion was replaced on the front by Second Battalion. More fierce fighting ensued. At one point the Germans counterattacked and some American soldiers thought the order was given for them to withdraw. It hadn't been and reversing their rearward momentum was a challenge.

"I can remember when somebody said to withdraw," he explains. "Everybody said, 'Move back! Move back!'"

But the American line held and a final German attack neared success once again until a five-minute barrage from division artillery stopped it. Afterward, the fighting diminished as glider troops from the east of Carentan joined the fight.

"After that we got to the edge of this hedgerow and the guys in front of us must have had luck because the Germans backed off," Labutka says. "We were involved in a lot of hedgerow fighting. A heck of a lot of it."

The hedgerows in Normandy were an obstacle underestimated by the Allies. For centuries farmers fenced their small fields with solid walls of earth, often four-feet high, and topped them with hedges whose tangled roots bound each row into a natural fortification. They were created to prevent erosion, but the Germans used them for lines of defense and counterattack. Many little battles were fought there at very close range. When attacking Americans approached one row, they found a strong force of defenders behind it and properly emplaced machine guns at both ends. If the enemy was dislodged or fell back, German troops behind another hedgerow went into action with mortars or artillery.

"Finally, we got in a line across this last hedgerow and went into Carentan. That's when I saw dead Germans stacked like cordwood. Honest to God! We were shooting blind into the town and when we got there their bodies were stacked up just like logs. The Germans themselves must have stacked them that way. Somebody did."

On June 12th, Carentan was declared clear of the enemy and the town was occupied. The final job for the 101st in Normandy was to maintain positions at the base of the Cotentin Peninsula. As June turned into July this area proved relatively quiet—manned largely by Allied patrols and inhabited mainly by wandering cows.

"It was about a month since the landing before we had a chance to get off the line," he says. "We had no change of clothes and no showers during that time, but afterward we were eating steak. We'd kill a cow and cook it over a fire. We had steak for breakfast and steak for dinner."

The 101st was relieved after thirty-three days of continuous combat and moved by trucks to an area behind Utah Beach on July 10th. The division history records that in little more than a month of combat, the division suffered 4,670 casualties. The paratroopers were taken to England by landing craft from July 11th to 13th and returned to their old quarters north of London. At least one month of back pay awaited them and leaves were approved. Labutka says most of the paratroopers who were given passes went to London to celebrate.

"I went to London to drink and diddle. Booze and women. Don't forget, I was just a kid."

The division was replenished and took part in more training during the next two months. More airborne missions were proposed but each time they were canceled due to the rapid Allied advance in France. The good life in England didn't last, however, as the 101st was slated to take part in a plan to liberate Holland. Dubbed Operation Market Garden and developed by Gen. Bernard Montgomery, British ground commander, it called for airborne forces (the Market phase) to drop behind German lines and secure a 100-mile corridor as British armor forces (the Garden phase) came up from Belgium to eliminate the German positions at Arnhem. Montgomery hoped the attack would bust an opening into the Ruhr Valley, Germany's industrial center, if it succeeded. But it didn't, and the bridge at Arnhem (at the far end of the corridor) became known as "A Bridge Too Far." Eisenhower was reluctant at first to support the mission, but eventually he relented. Bradley called it "the wrong plan at the wrong time in the wrong place."

The three parachute regiments of the 101st had separate assignments in Holland. Labutka's 502nd was charged with securing the landing zone near Eindhoven, capturing a bridge over the Dommel River and attacking the village of Best in order to secure the lower section of the British advance. Loaded with the same amount of equipment as in Normandy, the daylight drop into Holland was picture-perfect.

"It was nothing like Normandy. It went off like a practice jump. There was no opposition."

The only obstacle Labutka encountered in the jump was barbed wire, which gave him a cut above his right knee. The scar it caused has remained with him.

"They wanted to give me a Purple Heart," he says. "But I turned them down. Why should I accept a medal for a scratch when guys around me were getting killed?"

While the paratroopers had an uneventful flight from England and an easy drop, it was different for the division's glider troops. Of the seventy gliders that took part, only about fifty made it to Holland intact. Some landed far behind German lines, some were hit by flak, and some crashed upon landing due to obstacles planted in the fields.

"The Germans had sticks, trees actually, buried in the ground every ten feet which ripped those gliders apart," Labutka says. "Some of them contained jeeps and cannons and when they hit the poles there was equipment all over the place."

With the landing zone secured and the Dommel River crossed, the march on the bridge that crossed the Wilhelmina Canal at Best commenced. Just as intelligence reports of enemy troop strength at Carentan were in error, so it was here. The Germans who defended the canal bridge and Best were thought to be of poor quality and Allied planners anticipated that one company of paratroopers could do the job of taking both. But after finding the bridge heavily defended, another company was sent in. Later, both the Second and Third battalions joined the attack. At one point, Labutka's Second Battalion attacked across an open field and took serious losses from artillery, mortars, and machine guns.

"Some of our guys were bunched up," he explains. "I even yelled at them to scatter. You're never supposed to get close to the next guy. That's what they taught us—don't bunch up because that's what the enemy is looking for. Then a mortar shell hit three of them. One guy was hit right in his lap. Another one of them was dying. He had me recite the Act of Contrition to him. He died right there in my arms."

When the battle for Best ended, half of the 101st was engaged plus a column of British tanks.

"We captured about 200 German soldiers at Best, kids and old men. They just threw down their guns. Two guys with bazookas were taking them back to the rear when somebody said, 'Okay, we're moving.' So I was walking behind this machine gunner and he threw his machine gun over his shoulder and must have pulled the trigger. There was one shell in it and it hit my helmet, put a nick in it, and boy did I hit the ground. I gave him hell. I said, 'You're supposed to clear your gun.' He said, 'I thought I did.'"

After the fall of Best, the 502nd was ordered to hold defensive positions in the area.

"Up to this time I was still a private," Labutka says. "But shortly after Best I went, on one order, from private to Pfc. to corporal to sergeant to staff sergeant to tech sergeant. That's how many guys got wounded or killed. In one order I went from private to platoon sergeant. I had forty-seven guys under me—three rifle squads and a mortar squad. That's when I was issued a Thompson submachine gun.

"This one time in Holland," he continues, "I was looking through my field glasses and saw Germans about 100 yards away. They were squatted, with their pants down, crapping. So I radioed over to my mortar sergeant, Earl Rodd, and asked, 'Do you see that?' He said, 'How about me going back and laying a couple of shells in there?' I said, 'That's just what I want you to do when I let you know there are more Germans.' So he went back and I was on the radio with him and about five or six more of them came down. I said, 'Earl, lay a couple in there now.' He did. They were all tree bursts, hitting these big fir trees. Those Germans scattered all over. You should have seen them run with their pants half-way up. I laughed. I think it was the first time I laughed like that since I'd gotten over there."

It was also in Holland where Labutka had a chance encounter with the division's artillery commander, Brig. Gen. Anthony C. McAuliffe, who gained fame later with his "Nuts" response to a German surrender order at Bastogne. Following their Holland jump, the paratroopers were told to take off their prized jump boots and instead wear regular-issue combat boots lest, if they were captured, the Germans could identify them as airborne.

"One day, this was also after Best, General McAuliffe was walking by me and asked, 'How are your men eating, sergeant?' And we had just passed Third platoon, and they had a pig on a spit. I said, 'We're eating well, sir.' He said, 'So I guess you are.' And then he asked me, 'How do you like your combat boots?' I said, 'I hate them, sir.' He said, 'You do know why we can't wear jump boots?' I said, 'Sure, the enemy will know we're paratroopers.' He said, 'That's right, sergeant.'"

Whether German forces would have treated airborne troops (if captured) any differently from the regular infantry, Labutka says he isn't sure. But the switch of boots would be repeated again when the division was sent to Bastogne.

The main objective of Market Garden, an opening to the Ruhr Valley, never materialized. In that respect, the operation was a failure. On the plus side, however, the Allies drove sixty-five miles through German lines, crossed two major rivers, seized airfield sites and created a buffer to protect the port of Antwerp. By mid-November after seventy-two days of combat the 101st was moved to its base at Camp Mourmelon, a one-time French airfield, where paratroopers received passes to Paris, enjoyed good food and champagne, and experienced frequent USO performances.

"Bob Hope came one time. But that wasn't my cup of tea. I never went to a movie or saw a show. I was busy drinking and playing poker. I had to be the unluckiest poker player in the world. Maybe I drank too much when I played. But what else was there to do? There were no women around."

Once again the good times were about to end as German forces opened its last offensive in Western Europe through the Ardennes Forest in Belgium. Their attack, launched on December 16th, rolled through the sparsely held line of either inexperienced or battle-weary American troops. The 101st was soon in the "center" of the action.

"I was AWOL in Paris when they attacked," Labutka admits. "I had a pass, but it was overextended. You see, me and my first sergeant were close. He gave me a pass whenever I wanted one. All I had to do was sign somebody's name to it and show it to the bus driver. He didn't know one lieutenant from another. It was easy. So me and a buddy were in Paris. I think we'd been there four days and we were planning to visit the Folies-Bergere, the famous nightclub. But before we got there we stopped at this little outside cafe drinking gin and orange juice. We never got to the nightclub because somebody rolled us. It was probably one of the girls we met.

"So without any money we went back to Rainbow Corner. This was a place in Paris where all the G.I.s went. A lieutenant came by and said, 'Sergeant. I got bad news for you. Be at Rainbow Corner at 5 o'clock tomorrow morning.' I asked, 'What happened?' He said, 'Breakthrough.' There were about two truckloads of guys from our outfit in Paris and we went back to Mourmelon."

The surprise German attack easily knifed through the American lines. Poor visibility grounded Allied planes and over the next three days the situation worsened for the Americans. One option for Eisenhower was to commit his reserve units, one of which was the 101st. With its division commander in the United States and assistant commander in England, the job fell to Gen. McAuliffe to lead the paratroopers into battle. But this time they didn't drop from the air, they went on trucks and arrived in Bastogne on December 19th. This was the southern sector of the German thrust guarded in part by the tired U.S. Twenty-eighth Division which had been sent to that area for rest. It had seen action since just after the Normandy landings and more recently had been involved in the desperate fighting in the Huertgen Forest. The Twenty-eighth also contained men from Labutka's hometown National Guard unit. As the Germans advanced, the 28th fell back and the 101st moved in.

Courtesy of Ludwig Labutka

While on a pass to Nice, France, Labutka (left) and fellow paratrooper Howie Barasso of New England are pictured along the Riviera in March, 1945.

"Going into Bastogne I was in charge of two trucks," Labutka says. "That's when I heard that the National Guard from Pennsylvania was there. I knew guys in Company D from Butler, and naturally I knew guys in Company C from Ford City. So here they were, the Twenty-eighth Division, coming out of Bastogne while we were going in. One of the guys I knew I did see coming out, Pete Rhodes from Company C."

Once in Bastogne the 101st immediately set up a defensive perimeter in all four directions around the town, a radius of about sixteen miles. The town was soon encircled by German forces and Labutka found himself on the northwest side. It was the worst winter in years and temperatures frequently dropped below zero. When men touched a gun barrel their skin stuck to it. Snow was as constant as were American patrols to probe the German lines.

"We didn't go too far out on patrols," he recalls. "They just wanted to see how far the Germans were. This one time we were on patrol and my radio operator, Jimmy Agnostis, was behind me. I was up the field a way and I stopped because I thought I saw some German troops about 200 yards away. Then I heard this 'pow-pow' from behind me and damn if I wasn't hit in my helmet again! I said, 'Jimmy, you SOB! That's twice I almost got killed with our own guns!' He said, 'I'm sorry, I'm sorry.'"

Underestimating the division's resolve to defend the town, and overestimating their own ability to take it, four Germans approached the American lines south of Bastogne on December 22nd. One of them carried a white flag and another held a message that proposed the Americans, since they were surrounded, surrender. If the offer was rejected, the note promised that Bastogne would be destroyed by heavy guns. When the threat reached General McAuliffe his reaction was "Nuts." Thus, that answer was eventually delivered but the German envoy didn't understand its meaning. The American officer in charge said through a translator: "If you don't understand what 'Nuts' means in plain English, it's the same as 'Go to hell!'"

The German "bulge" through the Ardennes was reaching its high mark as the offensive ran low on supplies and met stiffer Allied resistance. By December 24th, Hitler was said to be so incensed that such a small town could be such a big thorn in the German drive that he ordered Bastogne be annihilated. While the Germans could have easily bypassed the town, they didn't and instead concentrated their efforts to the northwest where the 502nd was positioned.

"The Germans did bring in tanks and shot 88s into our Third platoon. They got hammered. For the most part, my platoon was in reserve. That's why I didn't get into contact with German tanks. But our Third platoon from E Company took it bad."

As Christmas neared the visibility cleared enough that Allied planes, at times flying 250 sorties a day, were able to drop supplies to the beleaguered paratroopers who were now running low on everything. Most airdrops reached American hands although some landed too far away. Labutka remembers celebrating the holiday with an ice cream-like concoction made by putting snow in a canteen cup and adding lemonade powder from dropped C-rations.

"When those skies brightened and I heard those planes coming over to give us ammunition, food, everything we needed, I thought that was the nicest Christmas present I ever got."

A U.S. armored division finally arrived from the south on December 26th and pushed its way into Bastogne a few days later. This corridor was eventually widened and on January 18, 1945, the 101st was poised to exit the town that it had called home for a month.

"We marched out of Bastogne and got on trucks," Labutka says. "Outside of town, somebody had put up this big sign: This Is The Battled Bastion of the Bastards of Bastogne."

Now on trucks once again the division was sent to Luxembourg and later to the Alsace region of France. Stationed there until mid-February the paratroopers saw little action. Afterward, they returned by train to their camp at Mourmelon where, on March 15th, the 101st became the first division in history to receive the Distinguished Unit Citation (now called the Presidential Unit Citation) as an entire division. Labutka remembers when General Taylor addressed the men and told them that when the war in Europe was over, he was going to have the division sent to Japan. It didn't go over too well.

"He said that, if possible, we were going to Japan and finish off the Japs. We weren't in the mood for that. Do you know what he heard? From the rear ranks: 'Boo!' Then louder: 'Boo!' Then finally from the entire division: 'Boo!' Can you imagine what that sounded like from a whole division?"

American forces by this time were east of the Rhine River and the division was ordered to Dusseldorf and then to southern Germany and finally to Bavaria. Its last mission was to capture Berchtesgaden where Hitler maintained his mountain home. It was May 8th and the war was over.

"We were billeted in a nice house," Labutka says. "At the time, people who owned the house could put their valuables in a room or on the third floor and lock it up. The house I was in was Eva Braun's house, Hitler's mistress. It had lots of big rooms, high ceilings, but little furniture because it was all locked up. So somebody from my platoon broke into one of the rooms and took a bunch of stuff, mostly jewelry. We had a meeting with the company commander the next day, and he said, 'We'll give you guys 'til reveille to put everything back. If not, there's going to be repercussions.'

"At 5:30 the next morning, nothing was returned. So the next day they made us go on a twenty-five-mile forced march with a full pack—rifle, blanket, no water. They said we were going to do that every day until everything was put back. That night, after our march, the guys who took the jewelry put it all back. Three or four guys were involved. We knew who they were and everybody wanted to beat them up. And they would have been beaten up if it had gone on any longer."

Labutka left Europe from the southern French port of Marseille on September 6th and arrived stateside eight days later. He was discharged on September 21st.

"I wouldn't take a million dollars to do it over again," he says. "And you couldn't give me a million not to have gone through it. I'm glad I went through it. I was lucky. The Lord took care of me because I'm still here. But I know one thing: I would never jump from an airplane again, unless somebody called me a chicken."

I WAS A MACHINIST MATE AT NORMANDY

by A. A. Leonard

I was a machinist mate at Normandy—one of a four-man landing barge crew. We were attached to the U.S.S. *Joseph T. Dickman*, APA-13. In 1944 the *Dickman* had already participated in the invasion of Fedhala, North Africa; Gilla, Sicily; and Salerno. She proudly displayed four German swastikas painted on her bridge, indicating she had shot down four German aircraft.

We spent the first five months of 1944 in northern Scotland engaging in war games that would eventually lead to the actual invasion. The latter part of May we sailed to the south of England where we embarked troops and material. The ship was sealed, no one allowed on or off. We knew this was to be the real thing. We received our final briefing the night of June 5th. After the briefing religious services were held. On a normal Sunday Catholic services were attended by fifteen to twenty hardy souls; however, on the night of June 5th both soldiers and sailors crowded the passage ways and ladders leading to the deck where services were being held, straining to hear the Chaplain's words.

A few hours later we weighted anchor and sailed for the coast of France. The English Channel was rough and the weather was wet and miserable. We reached our point of debarkation and within a few minutes, at 2:00 A.M., we loaded and lowered into the choppy waters twenty-seven LCVPs (Landing Craft Vehicle Personnel) and two LCMs (Landing Craft Mechanized), also known at Tank Lighters. We formed our individual boat waves and headed for the invasion beaches of Normandy.

On the way most of the troops became seasick—adding to the already uncomfortable feeling of being like sardines in a can. We reached our first line of departure only to find both guide boats had been hit and were bottom-side up with survivors standing on the keel giving us the go-ahead sign and "V" for victory sign. We were very proud to be Americans at that moment. We reached our final line of departure and after a few moments the wave commander gave the signal to run for the beach.

A few minutes before "H" hour all incoming gunfire ceased. This gave the Germans who had been hunkering down the opportunity to fire at us with a vengeance. As we approached the beach, we were able to see that some of our boats in the first wave had struck mines or had been hit by gunfire. Surviving shipmates were swimming to other boats to be picked up. We hit the beach and dropped the boat ramp. The troops left the barge and moved fast toward higher round. We raised the ramp and attempted to back off the beach. Unbeknownst to us, our bilge pumps had become clogged and water rushing in when our ramp was down caused us to be waterlogged. The coxswain put the engine in reverse and revved it up as fast as possible. To no avail—our boat would not budge. At that moment panic and fear set in. We were a stationary target and German gunfire was bracketing our boat. Boats on both sides of us were hit. I began to pray, making the most outlandish promises to God if only he would let me live. My whole life seemed to pass before my closed eyes. A few seconds later we could feel our boat slowly moving back off the beach. The coxswain swung the bow around and we headed out to sea and safety, German shells landing where we had been only moments before.

We made subsequent trips back to the Normandy beaches, but on that day, June 6th, we lost eight of our landing craft and several of my shipmates were killed or wounded. Also that day, in addition of Purple Hearts issued, several of our crew received medals for meritorious service.

After my discharge and return to civilian life, being a mere mortal, I soon forgot the promises I made to God that eventful day. However, each June 6th I take a few minutes to thank God for letting me live and to say a prayer for my shipmates who were killed during the invasion.

NORMANDY

D-Day, June 6, 1944, Operation Overlord began the liberation of France. In the pre-dawn darkness three entire airborne divisions fell on the German rear echelons to disrupt reaction to the main landings. Daylight revealed a fleet of 5,000 ships and virtually every aircraft in Allied possession in western Europe supporting troops hitting five beaches (Juno, Sword, Gold, Utah, and Omaha). Most of the landings went well, with the stunned German defenders unable to organize resistance. However, on Omaha beach the situation was so precarious that General Eisenhower had orders to withdraw the troops ready to be issued. After taking thousands of causalities the situation improved. And the order was never given.

The troops on Omaha were mostly Americans. By the end of the day they had secured their beachhead, and along with forces from the other beaches, began to move inland. Within days, Allied forces built up to over one million fresh, well-armed, men.

As the beachhead expanded inland, a major German counterattack began. It was late in forming and while executed well, it could not forestall the inevitable. On June 27th the port of Cherbourg fell into Allied hands. Once the port was cleared, the flow of men and supplies increased the pressure on the German army. Allied troops entered Paris on August 25th. By September, Anglo-American troops were preparing to enter Germany itself.

DAD WAS A PARATROOPER

by Jeff Bosworth

☆ ☆ ☆

☆ ☆ ☆ Training in England ☆ ☆ ☆

Dad was originally assigned as a heavy machine gunner in the 504th Parachute Infantry Regiment. Sometime during basic training, the army decided to create a new regiment, the 507th. Because Dad had taken some college courses in accounting, General Ridgeway asked him if he was interested in transferring over to the 507th as a supply sergeant. This prospect seemed much more appealing than lugging a heavy machine gun halfway across Europe, so he enthusiastically agreed.

One of the troopers (Sergeant Thompson) in Dad's outfit was a master mechanic with Caterpillar Tractors. After a considerable amount of experimenting, he was eventually able to modify the M1 carbine from a semi-automatic weapon to full automatic. Dad was one of only three men who were able to obtain this weapon. (The other two being the inventor and the CO.) The price to Dad was keeping the trooper in brand new uniforms, so he could always look sharp. As will be explained later, this was probably the best business deal my dad ever made.

By the time Dad saw his first action at Normandy, he had been in training for over two years (March 1942-June 1944). The men were tired of training and getting anxious to join the fight. Dad said that it was like being in spring training for a football team too long; you wanted to get started and see what you could do.

☆ ☆ ☆ D-DAY ☆ ☆ ☆

Dad was assigned to Headquarters Company, 1st Battalion, 507th Parachute Infantry. They left England for the Normandy peninsula during the early morning hours of June 6, 1944. At about 2:00 A.M. they were over Normandy, but still several miles from their assigned drop zone. A German antiaircraft shell ripped through their plane. Fortunately for the men inside, it was a timed fuse, and did not explode on impact, but went in one side and out the other. The plane was flying at only 400 feet, but the Germans had expected them to be much higher. As soon as the plane took the hit, the pilot turned on the green jump light and ordered everyone out of the plane, even though they were not yet to their drop zone. There is an old army joke about who would want to jump out of a perfectly good working airplane. Dad says after the shell went through the plane, no one wanted to stay inside. That and the plane wasn't perfectly good working.

Each trooper who jumped out of a plane was weighted down with his own body weight in equipment. Dad weighed about 185 at the time, but was over 300 pounds with all his gear. (Dad told me once that he stuffed all his pockets with rations, as he didn't want to go hungry behind enemy lines). Dad carried the following when he jumped on D-Day: three days' rations, a .45 pistol with four to seven magazines, two bandoleers of carbine ammo, two canteens, two ten-pound landmines, and two grenades (one gamma and one fragmentation).

Each plane carried an eighteen-man stick of troopers. Dad was the second highest rank in his stick, so he was last in line. There was not enough room for him in the body of the plane, so he was seated next to the navigator. Because of the lack of room, he was unable to hook up his static line with the others. He had to wait until the jump light was turned on, then hook up on the run toward the door. The eighteen-man stick was supposed to exit the plane in eleven seconds. They landed near Orglandes, on the road to Amfreville.

Because of the extra weight and the low altitude of the jump (400 feet), many troopers broke ankles on the hard landing. Dad said that he only had time to complete "half a swing" underneath his chute on the way down. Dad broke his right ankle when he landed with one leg in a foxhole.

At Lieutenant Law's order, Dad took over as Battalion Supply Sergeant as the original sergeant drowned during landing.

As a result of the heavy antiaircraft fire, most of the troopers of the 507th were heavily scattered. Dad was able to join up with eight other troopers by using his "cricket." One of the men asked my dad, "Hey sarge, do we play hide and seek now?" This brought on a brief laugh to relieve the tension, but no one would ever admit to saying it.

With the aide of these troopers, Dad managed to get to a near-by French farmhouse. The farmer's wife was a schoolteacher who spoke a little English. When Dad showed her the flag on his right shoulder, she jumped for joy. She invited all the men inside and hugged them each in turn. Then her husband offered Dad his old flatbed truck, and dug up a five-gallon can of gasoline he had buried in the back yard to keep from the Germans. Dad and Sergeant Carlucci signed a receipt for the truck so that the couple would be able to recover its cost from Uncle Sam. The two sergeants and about a half dozen other troopers boarded the truck and drove to Amfreville. My dad ordered the other men to take off their helmets, lie down in the back of the truck, and keep strict silence in order to remain undetected. The precaution was well founded, as during the trip they passed several German patrols. German anti-parachute troops riding on bicycles were using the same road. Dad says the Germans were so close he could have reached out and touched them with a yardstick. They also passed about 100 German troops who were lining up for breakfast. They were never detected and managed to join up with Lieutenant Colonel Timmes, the 2nd Battalion commander, at Amfreville.

☆ ☆ ☆ Normandy Campaign ☆ ☆ ☆

For the first several days after the landing, Dad was a part of the group led by Timmes. Dad was sent to check out a nearby farm-house. He crawled over one of the many hedgerows and came face to face with a pair of Germans who were setting up a machine gun. Both sides opened fire at the same time. A bullet from the machine gun hit my dad in the arm, passing all the way through, and flipping him over on his back. The thought "Oh my God, I'm dead!" raced through his mind before he lost consciousness. When he recovered, he crawled up to the hedgerow, and saw that it was covered with blood, but that there were no bodies. Dad always believed that he killed the loader and wounded the other. He also believed that his specially made automatic carbine saved his life.

Dad was in a bad way. He was still hobbled by a broken ankle and now he was unable to move his right arm. About this time Lieutenant Law showed up, and asked him if he could move. Dad wasn't sure he could continue, until they noticed machine gun bullets striking the trees over their heads. Law told him to put a hand-kerchief between his teeth, and follow him the best he could. Dad did as ordered, and made his way to a nearby farmhouse that was being used as an aide station. He spent the next few hours at the station, as he was unable to operate his weapon until he regained the use of his arm. While he was in the aide station a lieutenant borrowed his specially modified carbine, and he never saw it again.

Timmes had set up a defensive perimeter around the town of Amfreville. Their objective was to deny access of the road to the Germans, in order to keep them from reinforcing the beaches. The town was surrounded on three sides by swamps and other areas flooded by the Germans. The enemy tried to break through their lines for seven and a half days, but was never successful. The 507th was finally able to link up with the 90th Infantry division on D-Day plus eight. However, it was almost thirty days later before the regiment was fully reorganized with all the troopers who were fit for duty in the correct units.

It seems that a lot of the local French peasant girls soon were wearing petticoats made from U.S. parachutes! They went and dug them up after the landings.

A couple of days after D-Day Dad and several other troopers were crossing a field enclosed by hedgerows when they came under a mortar attack. A 60 mm. round hit a sergeant from B Company right in the helmet. Fortunately, the round was a dud. The round stuck in his helmet! The sergeant walked away with no serious wounds other than a very sore neck, muttering "Jeeze am I lucky!"

Another soldier was not quite so lucky. While crossing a flooded field, a comrade took a direct hit from an enemy artillery shell. The soldier was completely disintegrated.

Around seven to ten days after D-Day the outfit managed to liberate a small village. The Germans controlled the single road to the village. The road was raised and narrow, and bounded by water on both sides. Some of the troops found a boat and made several trips ferrying troops to a dry spot where they could flank the town. They captured it and used one of the houses as a supply center. Dad saw a glass of clear liquid on a table. As it turned out, it was a glass of cognac. The unexpected shock buckled his knees. They took several prisoners. They were allowed to keep their personal items, but Dad took a backpack (which I still have) and a pair of pistols. Although he carried these weapons throughout the rest of the war, they were confiscated by a desk-jockey lieutenant in New Jersey when he returned to the U.S.A. This was the second time he lost weapons to a lieutenant. When he told me this story again in 2000, he still was shaking his fist at this lieutenant. Dad said he yelled at him for not "even getting your feet wet you dirty #!@%!" Some of the troopers had to be physically restrained from attacking him.

☆ ☆ ☆ Citation ☆ ☆ ☆

Silver Star awarded for gallantry in action on July 7, 1944. Awarded by General Howell at Tollerton Hall Parade Ground. The official citation signed by General Ridgeway reads at follows:

DONALD E. BOSWORTH, 19083741, Staff Sergeant, 507th Parachute Infantry. For gallantry in action on 7 July 1944 about one-half mile from LITHAIRE, FRANCE. Sergeant BOSWORTH was acting as battalion supply officer when the First Battalion, 507th Parachute Infantry, moved into positions on the forward slope of a hill one-half mile south of LITHAIRE, FRANCE. Before the battalion could get well into position, it was pinned down by enemy fire. The battalion was in an extended position covering a front of about six hundred yards along a road under direct observation of the enemy who were in well dug in and well concealed positions about a hundred yards to the front. Word was soon passed down the line that Company "A," which was on the left flank, was nearly out of ammunition.

When Sergeant BOSWORTH received this word he immediately had a truckload of ammunition moved as far forward as possible by truck and from there he personally, with total disregard for his own personal safety, made several trips up and down this road, all the time being completely exposed to enemy fire, carrying ammunition of all kinds. Seeing that he was not getting enough ammunition to the Company by carrying it, he found a wheelbarrow and continued hauling it to the Company until the enemy were finally wiped out or forced to withdraw. It was largely due to his untiring efforts, and courage while under enemy fire that the mission of the battalion was finally accomplished. Entered military service from SACRAMENTO, CALIFORNIA.

Dad said he made three trips with the ammo. The men were using up their ammunition at an alarming rate. Dad says that the mortarmen were shooting twenty-two rounds before the first one hit the ground. The cook was the one who obtained the wheelbarrow. After it was all over, someone told him how close the enemy fire came to him, and Dad says he fainted.

☆ ☆ ☆ The 507th ☆ ☆ ☆
at the Battle of the Bulge

The 507th was recalled from England and sent to join the Battle of the Bulge as reinforcements. Dad was in a jeep as part of a convoy. His jeep had a .30 caliber machine gun. As they were travelling they were spotted by a German reconnaissance plane, which the GIs called a "Washing machine Charlie." As the plane passed overhead Dad and another trooper operating a .50 caliber machine gun out of a truck opened fire. Dad didn't have tracer ammunition, so he fired into the plane's path, and let the plane fly into his line of fire. Dad and the other trooper were given combined credit for a kill. After the plane went down in flames, an officer came over to reprimand Dad and the other soldier for giving away their position with their fire (as if the plane hadn't discovered their position!).

During this battle, my father and his comrades were often forced to eat frozen rations. Dad remembers that he had to use his knife to break the rations into small enough pieces to eat. The only warmth they had was from a small candle at the bottom of a foxhole. It was important to keep the foxhole covered with a poncho to keep from betraying your position to enemy artillery observers. The Germans could zero in on any target within seconds. One day twelve men form the mortar platoon decided that hey had enough of eating cold chow and decided to start a fire to have a warm meal. Within seconds this activity had the predictable result of the German artillery immediately zeroing in on their position with an artillery barrage. All twelve men were killed or wounded.

At one point Dad's outfit was part of a force assigned to capture the town of Houffalize, which he describes as a railroad center. They had trouble getting in, so they called for an air raid. The Allies sent in a 1000-plane raid, which leveled the town. Dad said that was the first time he really appreciated how much 1000 was.

☆ ☆ ☆ Battle for Germany ☆ ☆ ☆

As they neared Munster, Dad was a passenger in a jeep carrying a trailer full of ammunition. They rounded a corner and found a German tank in the road. Dad doesn't remember the type of tank anymore, other than the fact that the gun barrel was HUGE! Dad described it as having sloping armor, so it was probably a Panzer V "Panther." The tank fired right away, striking the jeep near the gas tank. The force of the blast blew both Dad and the driver out of the jeep. Dad was wounded in the leg by the shrapnel and rendered deaf for three days because of the noise. The driver was more seriously hurt. Fortunately for Dad, the tank was loaded up with an anti-tank shell, not an anti-personnel shell. Otherwise it is doubtful he would have survived.

On one occasion near Munster, Dad was part of a patrol out looking to take Germans prisoner. Dad was moving across a field toward a dugout, when he heard his buddy Art Sied yell out something in German. He then heard the sound of weapons clanking on the ground. Dad feels Art saved his life by ordering the Germans to surrender.

All U.S. soldiers feared the German 88 mm. gun. Dad says that it was not unknown for the Germans to target a single solider, and they were deadly accurate. On one occasion he was near headquarters of the second battalion. A truck was parked outside with a driver in it. An 88 shell suddenly struck the truck, hitting the driver full in the body as it passed through. Dad went over to help him, but it was too late.

Near the end of the war, he was involved in some street fighting. On one occasion he saw a wounded German grandmother sitting in the middle of an intersection. She had most of one leg blown off, and was bleeding very badly. Dad crawled up to her, and tried to do the best he could to help. He gave her his shot of morphine and poured his sulfa on the wound. He tried to stop the bleeding. He stayed there and held her hand while he waited for the medics to come and take her away. He found out later that she died.

Dad was near Dusseldorf when he heard the war ended. They were trying to capture the Krupp works. They liberated many Russian prisoners, who had been forced into slave labor, but the Russian political leaders refused to take them back.

GLIDERS IN WW II

When most people think of gliders at war, they picture the swarms of British and American aircraft silently slipping through the night skies of Normandy just before the troops hit the beaches at D-Day.

That certainly was the largest glider operation in the war, and in history. But it was not the only one. Gliders were used to insert troops throughout the war by both sides. As a matter of fact, the first use of gliders began hours before the war even began in Western Europe.

Remembering World War I, Belgium constructed a string of forts along their borders. While many of these forces faced friendly Holland, they were constructed with an eye towards Germany, on the far side of their neighbor.

The strongest of these fortresses was Eben Emal. It commanded key river and road traffic. It's thick concrete walls and heavy weapons could make sure nothing entered Belgium. But it had a flaw. There was a small parade ground on top of the fort. German gliders were tasked with the world's first airborne assault. Their mission: take the fort, silence its guns and open the door to Belgium . . . and France.

They succeeded. But that mission and every glider mission including Normandy took a heavy toll on the glider troops. By the war's end the cost in elite troops lost in these vulnerable aircraft could no longer be justified and gliders flew into history.

HARRELL WILSON TATE

by Robert K. Tate

D ad was assigned to the 114th Signals Intelligence Company attached to the Headquarters Group, U.S. Twelfth Army in Europe. Because of the sensitive nature of his job he was never on the front lines of combat, but he did have some experiences which he passed on to his family, two of which I will now pass on.

When the Battle of the Bulge began Dad's unit was in a small Belgian town, whose people had gone through years of German military occupation. Dad said the townsfolk were overjoyed when the Americans arrived and chased the Germans out, but their joy was not long-lived.

When the Bulge started Dad's group was quickly loaded into trucks and driven out of town, much to the consternation of the inhabitants of this town. Those poor people were certain the Germans would be back, and they were terrified at the possibility of German reprisals. Fear does strange things to people; Dad saw that firsthand as they were leaving town. All along the road, people were shouting and cursing the U.S. Army for deserting them; fortunately, nothing happened to those people.

After leaving town, Dad's unit drove for awhile, until eventually the trucks pulled off the road and hid in some thick woods. They stayed in the trucks and waited until the battle began to swing in their favor. While they were never in any danger from enemy troops, they were scared out of their wits by the lieutenant in charge of their truck, in whom they had little faith. Because of the sensitive nature of their work, all the trucks, but especially the intelligence equipment and code books in those trucks, were wired to large amounts of explosives, and the lieutenant had charge of the trigger. Luckily nothing happened, and when the shells stopped coming from the east they knew they were safe.

Another incident occurred very near the end of the war. Once again my dad found himself in a town, perhaps in Germany this time. The MPs had made certain areas of the town off-limits, with especially strict orders that American soldiers stay within the boundaries of the town. Dad, however, had other ideas.

While walking about he met a young woman who, with hand signs, body language, and broken English, convinced him to follow her…in truth my dad didn't need much convincing. So off they went through the town, then through the off-limits part of town, and finally all the way out of town and into the countryside. It was a rainy day so Dad had his carbine slung muzzle-down over his shoulder.

Once they were well out of town, the girl stopped next to a clump of bushes. At this point, two German soldiers rose up from behind the bushes, giving Dad the scare of his life. He was in such a rush to get his carbine off his shoulder and leveled at these two Germans that he did not realize they were standing there with their arms raised in surrender. He said these two guys were in pitiful shape; one was just a young boy and the other a middle-aged man. Both had old, ragged bandages on. These fine examples of Germany's last-ditch military reserve had talked this girl into going to town and bringing out an American soldier to whom they could surrender and who would safely escort them back to town.

Now Dad had a real problem on his hands. Here he was on the wrong side of the boundary, with a girl on one side and two German prisoners on the other. He was thinking he was really in trouble this time, but he couldn't walk away and leave these people out there, so he took them back to town. Upon reaching town, he walked his catch to within a block of the MP station, got them safely on their way to the MPs, then ran like the devil in the other direction.

The story ended in a funny-sad way. Dad was never able to suppress his curiosity for long; soon he returned to the MP station. There, sitting on the curb, with MPs and other GIs walking all around them and ignoring them, were his two Germans. He never knew what happened to them; he guessed they were eventually picked up and processed as POWs before being released at war's end. At least they survived, and Dad was content to think he played a small—and unknown—part.

Dad passed away on August 24, 1999, after eighty-two adventurous years. He is buried in San Antonio, Texas, next to Louise, his wife of fifty-two years.

THE BULGE

In December, 1944, the German army made a last desperate bid for victory in western Europe. They formed an army of twenty-five divisions. They included new Panzergrenadier divisions created around cores of battle-hardened veterans with new recruits taken into service by extending the draftable age range to take young teenagers and older men to fill out their rosters.

Attacking on a fifty-mile front, the German army pushed American forces back into Belgium. Before they were stopped, they had created a deep salient. This bulge in the line is where the battle gets its name.

The Germans planned on breaking through to the beachhead at Normandy and throwing the Allied armies out of western Europe. They came very close to achieving their goals. Stubborn resistance and raw courage was enough to slow the momentum of the German army until American forces could regroup and begin to fight their way back onto the offensive. In mid-January 1945, in some of the worst winter storms in recorded history, the Bulge collapsed. The remnants of the German army retreated beyond the Rhine River into Germany.

COMBAT AND RECON
by Herbert G. Erhart

After three days on a train from Le Havre, France, we were let off at another replacement camp. We could hear artillery firing and realized we were getting closer to the front. This camp was in Givet, France, a little finger of land sticking into Belgium. Boy was it cold but the tents were dry, had cots, were heated, and the meals were hot. We stayed there three days and then entrained again and traveled back through France halfway to Paris and were offloaded then finally assigned to an outfit. I was assigned to Company "E," Second Battalion, 271st Regiment of the Sixty-ninth Infantry Division. In World War I, there was a regiment from New York called "The Fighting 69th" and a movie had been made starring Pat O'Brien and James Cagney. The Sixty-ninth, now a division, had taken the sobriquet, "The Fighting 69th," from that famous New York regiment.

What a change; we were genuinely welcomed, told to drop our packs, given a good hot meal, and then assigned to our platoon. We felt like human beings again instead of being treated like cattle going to slaughter. Of course, we were still cannon fodder even if treated better. The Sixty-ninth had been organized and trained at Camp Shelby, Mississippi, and then sent to Winchester, England, where they were when the Battle of the Bulge started. Many divisions were hit hard with casualties before the counter offensive so the 69th was stripped of a lot of their personnel as replacements. The remainder were shipped to France. The replacements I came over with were to bring the division back up to strength. We were near a French town named Liesse-Gizy (we called it Lizzy-Gizy).

I had hardly settled in and was trying to get acquainted with the other members of my platoon when a lieutenant came around asking for volunteers for a battalion combat and reconnaissance patrol. It seems that every battalion in the Sixty-ninth had been ordered to form one. They were trying to get five from each of the three line companies and five from the heavy weapons company plus three non-commissioned officers and of course one commissioned officer. We got only eighteen including the non-coms. I had no attachment to Company "E" as yet and I volunteered as I was "Going to be a hero." We loaded our gear in a 6 by 6 truck and after a number of hours were dumped off in some woods facing a town called Blankenheim as I remember. We had passed through Malmady where about 125 GIs had been executed by the Germans during the early days of the Battle of the Bulge and their bodies had been discovered and removed not long ago. This in turn led to some retaliation by GIs toward captured Germans which I condemn, but it certainly stiffened the spine of many GIs who otherwise might have considered surrendering to the Germans when things got "sticky."

We were relieving the Ninty-ninth Division on the Seigfried Line. The Ninty-ninth had been hit rather hard with casualties during the Battle of the Bulge. Our C & R Patrol was placed behind the line companies near where the kitchens, mail clerks, engineers, artillery, and battalion headquarters were located. We didn't have to dig a foxhole there and throughout the war I never did dig one. Now this was January and there was cold, snow, and drizzling rain and the ground was wet. Different guys paired up. I really didn't know anybody and seemed to be all alone. I borrowed an axe from the Engineers and built a "U" shaped wall about 30" high and about 7' x 5' out of small trees. A little Italian-American named Pericco asked if he could share my shelter and a buck sergeant also asked. I agreed as we needed all three shelter-halfs to cover the roof. I used a lot of small tree limbs to build a cushion off the wet ground and I kept us dry for the time we were there. The sergeant was a coward and deliberately got "trench foot" to get off the C & R Patrol. Obviously his first sergeant had "volunteered" him to get rid of him, a not uncommon practice.

We made a number of night patrols to check for mines, depth of the streams, and location of sentries. We were more worried about coming back to our own lines than going through the German lines. The green troops of the Sixty-ninth were really trigger happy. On our first night patrol as we were approaching our own lines, we heard a shot, then someone calling in English that he was shot and for someone to come and save him. It seems he was a roving patrol between two company lines and had been hit as he approached one company. Not knowing this at the time, we were not allowed to go to his aid. Our lieutenant was afraid it could be a German trick. He lay out there all the rest of the night. I don't believe there was a German within a mile of him.

We patrolled for about a week and our artillery shelled Blankenheim all the while. Then the attack began. Our patrol was split with half going with the battalion commander, a lieutenant colonel, and the other half with the executive officer (XO), who was a major—kinda like body guards with no real specific duties now that the attack was in progress. I was with the half with the XO.

The big push to the Rhine River was on and we were never in one place for more than twenty-four to forty-eight hours. Until the Rhine was reached, we made mostly night patrols, coming back in the early a.m. and passing information we had gathered to the lead company going in to the attack. This worked very well and the push forward also went very well. While the line companies rotated the lead and reserve positions, we were the only C & R Patrol so we were always busy. We crossed the Rhine on the "longest pontoon bridge in the world" near Sinzig, Germany. After that we were in the lead out in front of the battalion about two hours away, moving fast. The general attack overall was moving quickly and we were now motorized. We had a German fire truck—built more like a van than an American fire truck—in which we had our gear, "C" or "K" rations, and extra ammo. We also had a Jeep with a pylon for our machine gun. We didn't see another GI for days, but were always in touch with battalion headquarters by radio. The general orders were to see if the way was clear for the battalion to move forward fast. If we hit opposition, we were to handle it if we could, or hold until the battalion could move up to support us, or pull back if the enemy was too strong. Our position was analogous to putting your hand under a power lawn mover to see if the motor was running. We were there to draw fire and let battalion know that there was organized resistance ahead. Actually it worked very well, at least we were lucky. We weren't always able to handle the opposition we ran into, but we never backed up or pulled out.

I've no idea where we were, but one day the battalion was scheduled to advance up one road and cross a stream. The Germans had blown the bridge so the engineers were attempting to build a new bridge over the stream but were under shell fire from the other side. Apparently the Germans didn't have any howitzers and were using their 88s and shooting over a hill to try to knock out the bridge the engineers were putting across. The 88 is one hell of a good gun and we didn't have anything near as good until late in the war, but it is a high velocity, flat shooting weapon, and not very good used as a howitzer to lob shells over a hill. The Germans, however, were getting quite close to the bridge with this weapon, and battalion was sure they must have an observation post on our side of the hill to direct their fire so well with the kind of gun they were using. We were called upon to cross the river on remnants of the old bridge and find and knock out that observation post. On the hill there was a railroad switchyard cut into the side. We were moving toward where we thought the observation post had to be and down the switchyard when the Germans opened up with machine guns. We all dived into a convenient ditch not realizing at first that the Germans were looking straight down the ditch. They opened up again and the biggest man in the patrol who carried the 36 lb. machine gun was hit and out of action, and Pop McGuire, the oldest man in the patrol, had a bullet take a small piece of flesh out of his right thumb that was just in front of his head when he hit the ground. We called in mortar fire and blew that observation all to hell. Sergeant Parks went over to the edge of the switchyard to holler down that the observation post was no more, and was promptly shot by our own troops below. He was shot in the chest and I was the first man to him and opened up his shirt and saw two bluish areas where the bullets had hit in the chest just over the heart on the left. He lay there for about a minute and then said "Hell, I don't feel so bad" and started to get up, but I wouldn't let him and called for the medics who hauled him off. We found out later that the bullet must have been almost spent of its velocity. One hole was the entrance wound, the other the exit, and his ribs had deflected the bullet back out. How lucky can you get?

V-1

by Marjorie Elliott

☆ ☆ ☆

I REMEMBER -
ON JUNE 30TH - 1944
AT 2PM. A V-1 CRASHED
BUSH HOUSE - ALDWYCH
LEAVING ME UNDER DEBRIS -
100 KILLED - 100'S INJURED
I WAS WORKING FOR BRITISH
FOREIGN OFFICE . BLOOD
AND BODIES ALL AROUND
I WAS A BRITISH TEENAGER.

IN SURREY WHERE I
LIVED - 20 MILES FROM
LONDON - NEAR THE
CHANNEL WE WERE CALLED
BUZZ BOMB ALLEY.
WE GOT THE BOMBERS
COMING AND GOING .
WE WERE BOMBED OUT
TWICE.

REMEMBER THE
WONDERFUL FIREMEN
DURING THE TERRIBLE
FIRESTORMS OF THE BLITZ

REMEMBER THE
WONDERFUL CIVILIANS
BOMBED DAY AND NIGHT
FOR 7 MONTHS WHEN
WE STOOD ALONE

REMEMBER NIGHTS
IN THE HOME. TOO
TIRED TO GO INTO THE
SHELTER · NO SLEEP.

REMEMBER D-DAY-
LIVING ON THE COAST
ROAD WATCHING THE
TANKS ETC GOING
SOUTH - LOTS OF BRITISH
AND CANADIANS.

REMEMBER MY DEAR
MOTHER LINING UP FOR
HOURS FOR EXTRA RATIONS
AND THOSE WOMEN KEPT
THEIR PLACE IN LINE
EVEN WHEN THE SIRENS
SOUNDED ·

Courtesy of Marjorie Elliott

Marjorie Elliott

WE MET MANY YANKS
SOME WERE NICE. THEY
ALL HAD "A RANCH
AND A CADILLAC".

YES!. I REMEMBER
AND BECOME VERY
SAD - REMEMBERING
FRIENDS WHO DID
NOT COME BACK.
YOUNG LIKE ME BUT
FORGOTTEN BY TODAYS
YOUNG PEOPLE.

NEARLY 6 YEARS
OF WAR IN ENGLAND.
TERRIBLE YEARS
BUT THE BEST YEARS
OF MY LIFE ! WHEN
PEOPLE WERE SO
WONDERFUL AND
COMPASSIONATE
MAYBE BECAUSE
WE NEVER KNEW
IF WE WOULD BE
DEAD NEXT DAY.

REMEMBER THE STUKA
THAT DIVE BOMBED THE
TOWN OF STREATHAM
MOST FRIGHTENING SOUND -
I SHALL NEVER FORGET.

YEARS OF BLACKOUT -
YEARS OF POTATOES TO
EAT. SHABBY CLOTHES

I REMEMBER YOUNG
PILOTS WITH EARS AND
EYELIDS BURNS. KNOW
FEW YANKS - THAT
ONE AMERICAN WAS
KILLED IN THE "BATTLE
OF BRITAIN" HE IS
BURIED IN WESTMINSTER
ABBEY. WE BURIED
HIM WITH KINGS.

A LIBERATOR SAGA
by H. Ben Walsh

In June 1943, the 389th Bomb Group, together with the 44th and 93rd Bomb Groups, was placed on detached service from the Eighth Air Force in England to the Ninth Air Force in the Libyan desert. Major targets to be attacked by this B-24 Liberator force included Rome, Ploesti, and Wiener-Neustadt.

The July 19, 1943 raid on the Littorio marshaling yards in Rome was carefully planned so that no damage would be done to the religious and cultural sites in and around the Italian capital. Pilots and aircrew were given special instructions for a week studying detailed large-scale maps of the city. Bombardiers were specifically instructed that, in no case, should a bomb-run of less than one minute be made.

Brig. Gen. Uzal Ent briefed the crews in the pitch-blackness of our pre-dawn takeoff and once again stressed the importance of bombing accuracy.

Our takeoff and climb was uneventful and our assembled formation settled down for this 2,000 mile flight at 19,000 feet altitude. As we were nearing Messina, which was known as a hotbed of Luftwaffe fighters, I was informed by my engineer, T. Sgt. Orville Cain, that our fuel-transfer valve had failed and there was no possibility that we could continue the mission. I decided the only alternative for us was to abort the flight and head for Malta, the nearest friendly base available to us.

Within minutes of breaking formation, we were attacked by six FW-190 and ME-109 fighters diving out of the sun. I immediately put the plane in a vertical dive for the Mediterranean Sea. The length of time we spent in that dive seemed excruciatingly long with the fighters scoring repeated hits throughout the aircraft. As we were going through 8,000 feet, one ME attacked from three o'clock high and T. Sgt. James Stokes, right waist gunner, poured a withering fire at him at about 200 yards, causing the aircraft to burst into flames and crash into the sea. A second ME attacking from the same general direction was destroyed by Cain, firing from the top turret.

During these attacks, one 20 mm. shell exploded in the cockpit, which splattered me with fragments in the shoulders and neck. However, although the copilot, Lt. Samuel Blessing, saw the blood and knew that I had been hit, I really at the time felt no pain. I was busy holding the aircraft at just wave-top altitude in order to give us the maximum advantage in this fight. For some twenty minutes the fighters made approximately forty individual attacks on our plane. S. Sgt. Charlie Terry, left waist gunner, was badly wounded and lying on the deck. He was immediately replaced by S. Sgt. Ralph Peterson, the ball turret gunner who had climbed out of his turret which had been shot out of commission.

Two fighters continued pressing their attacks from nine o'clock with the leader seemingly intent upon ramming our aircraft. We were firing everything at him and he exploded about thirty yards from us. A fourth fighter, attacking from six o'clock, was destroyed by the tail turret gunner, S. Sgt. Art Farnham, in a firing duel which burned up his own turret guns. The two remaining fighters, probably reaching their own fuel endurance, turned away, ending the fight.

☆ ☆ ☆ The Bailout and Rescue ☆ ☆ ☆

Because of the damage in the bomb bay area, a bailout from the bomb bay (the normal exit for the aircrew positions in the front of the aircraft) was impossible. As a result, all crew members were ordered to make their way to the back of the ship and exit from the camera hatch located just to the rear of the waist guns. I knew there was no way that I would be able to make my way through that bomb bay with my chute on, so I slipped out of it and asked the copilot to leave it by the exit hatch.

With the bailout alarm bell ringing, I trimmed the aircraft as well as possible and made a dash through the bomb bay, threw on my chute, and bailed out. Looking down, I knew I was somewhat distant from the island, but what I didn't know was that the ocean current was not in my favor. After hitting the water, I activated my Mae West but it had so many holes in it that it was useless. As a result, I spent the rest of the afternoon alternately swimming and floating on my back, hoping against hope that I would be able to make shore before nightfall.

As the sun was beginning to set on the horizon, I realized my time was running out. There was no way I would be able to last the night, what with fatigue setting in and knowing sharks frequented the area. As my hopes were beginning to sink, I spotted a ship on the horizon heading in my direction. I, always the optimist, felt certain it must be a friendly and must be looking for me. However, as it got closer, it was obvious that the ship's course was taking it away from my position. At that moment, I realized this was my only opportunity for survival. In desperation, I gathered up all my strength and tried to literally leap out of the water, at the same time frantically waving my arms. This was my last and only chance!

Through great fortune and timing, and by the grace of God, the watch on the bridge spotted the white of my underarms reflecting from the setting sun against the dark green water. My heart skipped a beat or two when I saw the ship turn port and head for my position. I was pulled out of the water like a drowned rat by a sailor with a grappling hook. The captain of the ship (British) immediately gave me a large measure of rum which rendered me docile as a lamb. Then he proceeded to operate on my neck and back, removing the shell fragments. I could feel him working me over, but I was beyond pain.

The ship took me to Malta where we docked under blackout conditions. A small crowd had gathered having learned of my rescue and I was given a "Jolly Well Done, Yank" as they carried me to the waiting ambulance.

At midnight the Luftwaffe arrived overhead and gave Malta a pounding. I lay in my hospital bed hoping this day, July 19, 1943, would soon end and I could have a little rest.

I have relived this day so many times that every detail seems to be permanently etched in my brain. By all accounts, we should never have survived this battle. Many of the crew were subsequently killed. The only surviving crew member, in addition to myself, is the bombardier, Lt. Leo McBrian, who is living in Ripon, California.

THE AIRCREW ON THIS MISSION CONSISTED OF:

PILOT 1st Lt. H. Ben Walsh
COPILOT 2d Lt. Samuel Blessing
NAVIGATOR 1st Lt. Alvin Sheard
BOMBARDIER 1st Lt. Leo McBrian

ENGINEER T. Sgt. Orville Cain
ASST. ENGINEER S. Sgt. Charlie Terry
RADIO OPERATOR T. Sgt. James Stokes
ASST. RADIO OPERATOR Sgt. Wm. Jacobson Jr.
AERIAL GUNNER S. Sgt. Ralph Peterson
GUNNER S. Sgt. Arthur Farnham

In recognition of my "extraordinary achievement while participating in aerial flight on 19 July 1943," I was awarded the Distinguished Flying Cross. I was also awarded the Purple Heart "for wounds received in action on 19 July 1943."

It was quite a day.

STRATEGIC BOMBING

A city could die in a single night. When thousands of British planes came by night and more thousands of American bombers visited a German city by day, they left a city that could no longer support the Nazi war effort. Where factories, rail-heads, mills and transportation hubs were, only rubble remained.

It came with a high cost. Until late in the war, Allied fighters could not match the range of the big Liberators, Flying Fortress, and Lancasters. Until long-range P-47 Thunderbolts and P-51 Mustangs reached the air war, the toll German ME-109s, FW-190s and later, the ME262 jet fighters took was almost enough to protect German cities.

It is argued that strategic bombing can't destroy a nation's will to fight. Certainly, the German Luftwaffe could not take Britain out of the war during the Battle of Britain. German war production during the air raids rose to heroic levels. But they could not sustain the constant loss of equipment and personnel. Combined with a multi-front land war and overwhelming control of the air, the Allies were demonstrating that no part of the Third Reich was safe.

A TAIL GUNNER'S TALE

REMINISCENCES OF A B-17 TAIL GUNNER'S WORLD WAR II EXPERIENCES

by Russell A. Brant

☆ ☆ ☆

☆ ☆ ☆ The 379th Bomb Group ☆ ☆ ☆

Our crew was assigned to the 327th Squadron of the 379th Bomb Group at Kimbolton, England. We discovered that we had been assigned to a B-17 outfit in the First Division, there being a shortage of B-17 crews and excess of B-24 crews (for which we had been trained). Thus, when we arrived at the 379th we went into a quick training program to convert all of us to the B-17. Nearly all the crew were a bit leery of this move, except the copilot Ray Powers. He was jubilant as he had trained on B-17s before joining us at the Replacement Training Unit (R.T.U.) and trusted it much more than he did the B-24.

Major Creole (I am not sure of the spelling), the squadron commander, took charge of the retraining in late November of 1944, and we were an operational crew in about two weeks. The basic effort was to get Johnson checked out on take offs and landings with the entire crew in company for its orientation to its new environment. We all stood by our regular stations and I always kept the intercom on. Notable were the major's coachings, particularly on landings with: "Get the tail down, get the tail down, Johnson." The B-17 is a "tail dragger" with three point landings that include the tail wheel, as opposed to the B-24s where the three-point landing is with a nose wheel. These words of guidance were heard several times.

The time until we became operational gave us a chance to acclimatize to the environment, the routines, and get acquainted with fellow crews. During that first week I met two gunners from the squadron who were on crutches recovering from broken legs. "Boy," I thought, "here are a couple of aerial veterans with injuries to boot." While I was talking with them, I asked how they were wounded and they said, "We weren't wounded. We broke our legs when we scrambled off the chow truck." Eventually both returned to combat duty.

On days that a bombing mission was flown a regular ritual with ground personnel and stood-down air crews was "sweating out" the returning planes. That ritual was watching how many were returning the first pass over the field and what developed as they approached and landed. Red flares fired from a plane on the approach indicated wounded on board. Occasionally a damaged plane would ground loop on touchdown or the propeller from a windmilling engine would break from the shaft. These were fairly infrequent events during my tour of duty. I saw much more in the way of damage, loss, and injury while flying the combat missions: midair collisions, many near misses, frozen feet, and flak wounds—not to mention the view of damage and the implication of injury and death on the ground.

Courtesy of National Archives

B-17 OVER GERMANY

☆ ☆ ☆ Combat Flying ☆ ☆ ☆

Our crew's combat flying began with a briefing and a new arrangement. R. L. Johnson became our copilot and we got a new pilot, George. That virginal combat flight began quite normally with the airplanes assembling into squadrons and group. The flight was to take us to the Ruhr

Valley. Even before we arrived at the Initial Point (I. P.), beginning the bomb run to the target, we had engine problems with detonation and power loss. Perspectives from the tail position included seeing a series of large smoke rings being left in our wake. Another was hearing "Get me sixty inches" from the pilot to the engineer. (This was the pressure in inches of mercury required from the superchargers to maintain power.) I had not seen our flight (planes from our squadron, now ahead of us) for some time. Before arriving at the target area the pilot decided to abort the mission and head for home. We dropped our bombs at a designated bomb disposal area in the North Sea and returned to our base.

We had no sooner landed and parked when we were met by top brass from the 379th headquarters. These included the base operations officer, the engineering officers, and the ground crew chief to investigate the plane's aborted flight. They took the pilot along for a test flight. All systems proved to be functioning normally. The repercussion was that George was relegated to permanent copilot. George was referred to, in sotto voce, as "Fearless George." Later, the flight engineer told me that it was probably his mistake because he overlooked turning on the carburetor heat, realizing the error only in retrospect. This oversight deprived the engines of their potential. I suppose he should have come forward with the information, but we had little confidence in George as a pilot. The entire crew welcomed the prospect of Johnson's return.

☆ ☆ ☆ Flak Suits ☆ ☆ ☆

One evening one of our returning planes crashed in southern England, and the ground crew salvaged much equipment and parts. Flak suits were among the array. Thus, when the replacement plane arrived, and was being set up for combat, it had extra flak suits. In flight I sat on mine. However, all was not clear on the issue of this added protection.

One day we had a heavy bomb load and the fuel tanks topped off. While we were climbing to the bombing altitude, Johnson called me on the intercom to shed my spare flak suit and take it to the radio room, so the plane's load would be better balanced. Shortly after, he called again requesting the same for my regular flak suit. Even this was not enough. He then had me string out the contents of the two ammunition boxes onto the fuselage floor on either side, just forward of my tail position. Although spread out, this continuous string of ammo was still available for the guns. Still too much weight aft. I then went forward to the radio operator's compartment and waited until we arrived at the I. P. to return to the tail. This seemed to work all right; we got to the top of our climb in good shape. We reached the I. P. and I returned to my station for the short period of potential anxiety for the bomb drop.

I was surprised, maybe bemused, with our navigator for the day, a bombardier "retreaded" as a navigator. He was replacing our regular navigator for the mission. We were returning from the Berlin area and our track was paralleling the coast but well inland so the low countries and their coasts were in clear view. While we were going by one of the cities the pilot called the navigator and asked "What town is that?" The immediate reply was "Give me a minute." Minutes went by and Johnson again asked and the reply was "I'm checking, I'm checking." After a short additional interval I called the pilot on the intercom saying "Pilot, this is the tail and the town is Antwerp." There was almost an immediate confirmation from the "navigator."

☆ ☆ ☆ Reunion with My Father ☆ ☆ ☆

One day in March, after returning with the crew from a three-day leave in London, I found a telegram from Daddy awaiting me. It said that his ship was in at Liverpool and gave the name of the dock. When I approached Major Creole to ask for additional leave, he granted it for the entire crew for three days: so that I could enjoy a visit with Daddy, and our crew's continuity would not be broken. (After I left for the service my Dad had taken a refresher course, renewed his Merchant Marine Mate's license, and gotten a ship.) I caught the next train for Liverpool.

I met Daddy on his liberty ship midmorning the next day. Their cargo was fresh oranges, shipped in a new bulk method. I spent the next two days on board taking meals with the crew, and fine meals they were. It was not that our base fare was bad, but a change was welcome. Daddy and I had long talks and we had generally good chats with the crew at mealtime. I was amazed that some of the men professed disbelief that we were indeed flying over Germany and dropping bombs, and I don't think they were pulling my leg. We went into Liverpool and saw some of the sights, but our mission was to find a ship's chandler so that Daddy could buy a new sextant. We found one and he traded in his old sextant. The batteries in the light of this instrument were still functional more than ten years later. This was a signal occasion because it was my last real visit with Daddy.

We did not make a connection again until nearly a year later at home while he was dying of cancer.

Courtesy of Russell A. Brant

WITH FATHER IN LIVERPOOL
March 1945, on board his ship

☆ ☆ ☆ Bomb Runs ☆ ☆ ☆

My most memorable mission, except for the thirty-fifth, was on February 4, 1945, to Berlin. Our group was the lead for the entire maximum effort that day. We were the high-element lead of the leading squadron of the effort that included the First, Second, and Third Air Divisions of the Eighth Air Force. Approximately 1,000 bombers from the Eighth flew the daylight phase, followed by a similar number from the Royal Air Force (R.A.F.) that continued the assault during the late day and into the night.

As we made our way on the track in, I saw ever more aircraft in the clear air. As I looked back it reminded me of a cartoon depicting hornets emerging from a distant nest. The flak intensified as we advanced to the Potsdamer Platz and central Berlin targets, airfield and railhead. But we came out with no serious damage and no injuries. Some time later we saw the tag-end of our effort. Just behind, faint in the lower haze and far below, was the beginning of the R.A.F. effort.

Flak was our greatest concern, as most of Goering's Luftwaffe was destroyed or grounded for lack of fuel. Most of the flak around cities was of the 40 and 88 mm. variety; while it created damage and injury it was not greatly feared. But when the target was the Ruhr Valley we encountered 105 mm. guns. These black blasts had dramatic glowing-red centers and were much more effective than the smaller guns.

We got a nearby blast one day and the copilot yelled "I've been hit." Soon a clarifying signal indicated the flak had penetrated his glove and stung his hand without the letting of blood.

More often than not, fire from the lighter guns came in stacks of four shots spaced fifty feet apart (vertically) from each gun battery; target areas had from one to hundreds of batteries. On one trip we counted 200 holes in the stabilizers that surrounded the tail gun position. The ground crew chief wondered if I carried a rabbit's foot.

Another time, coming back from the Bavarian area and over the front lines, we ran into a fair concentration of flak. As I was peering out over the horizontal stabilizer, a six-inch hole suddenly appeared. Fortunately, the shells were set for altitude and not for contact detonation.

There was often a singular flak battery mounted on a rail car on the Netherlands peninsula that was known as "Pistol Pete" to the gunners. It was said that the damage inflicted from this defense occasionally turned back a plane.

☆ ☆ ☆ My Thirty-fifth Mission ☆ ☆ ☆

I saw very little in the way of enemy aircraft during my service, but there was still considerable potential. One mission, titled "Meatball," was made in cooperation with fighter groups attacking Luftwaffe bases. We scattered cluster bombs over an area of an enemy airfield, holding down the antiaircraft gunners while the fighters destroyed the planes on the ground.

On our thirty-fifth and last mission I saw a kaleidoscope of activity. Near the target area was flak and in the distance I saw a red and black fireball that was so large that it could only be an exploding aircraft. At six o'clock high, and higher than any of our fighter cover, a group of six bandits appeared as dots making contrails. I reported to the pilot and continued to watch, ready for attack. The dots and contrails disappeared, then the next thing I sensed was the crackle of .50 calibers. I saw an ME-262 pointing right at our squadron, coming in fast from six o'clock low. I zeroed in on him, firing with the rest of the tail guns. I probably did not get more than fifty to a hundred rounds off, but all the tail gunners were firing and some of the ball turrets as well. Among all of this clamoring Johnny yelled "there go two of Molesworth," as the ME-262s had shot down two of the 303rd bomb group's planes. The attacking ME-262 broke his climb off between us and our wing man and then it exploded just ahead of us. So the squadron got credit for downing one enemy aircraft.

As we were crossing the channel on the outbound leg that day I tested my guns as the regulations required. It was hard to ignore that the right-hand gun barrel was burned out, because it allowed an orange flame of about four or five inches to exit the muzzle. I thought little about it at the time, except to report it. Later, I realized that when we were engaged in combat at high altitude the flame must have been a foot and a half long. I have often wondered whether my gun's extended flame scared the wit out of the German pilot. Perhaps he thought it was a new weapon.

SEE Y'ALL
AFTER THE WAR

by Milton J. Elliott III

L t. Benjamin Grande Williams wasn't supposed to fly that day but when he learned the B-17s were going to tackle an oil refinery about fifty miles from Berlin, he volunteered for the mission.

He flew P-51s for the 357th Fighter Squadron of the 355th Fighter Group of the Eighth Air Force and was stationed at Stepple Morden Air Base near Cambridge, England. As "Little Friends," the group's first responsibility was to protect the bombers from Luftwaffe fighter attack and to shepherd home battle-damaged "Big Friends." A secondary assignment was to roam the enemy country-side, bombing and strafing targets of opportunity—from trains to airdromes to troop convoys.

Williams had logged forty combat missions and was credited with two kills, both targets of opportunity: he shot down a pair of ME-109s just as they were taking off from a Luftwaffe airfield.

On December 5, 1944, the routine was unchanged; it was a typical day. "We were up around 4 A.M., had breakfast, went to the briefing, collected our flying gear, and were taken by jeep to the flight line," Williams said. "My crew chief said everything was okay and we took off through the usual overcast, two in formation."

They assembled above the fog and mist at "an altitude of around 20,000 feet. My plane was a P-51D, with bubble canopy and had my fiancée's name, "Miss Ann," painted on the nose.

"After crossing the North Sea, we had an uneventful flight deep into Germany, protecting the '17s from attack by bandits without any encounters. As we continued flying over Germany at 21,000 feet, my plane started developing engine trouble. White puffs of smoke started coming out of the right exhaust stacks and some smoke began sifting into the cockpit.

"In a short while, the engine quit, the cockpit filled with smoke and

I dropped into the overcast. I had been in touch with my wingman and told him, 'I'm getting out of this damn thing, see y'all after the war.'

"With smoke still in the cockpit and being in the overcast, it was a tough job getting out. After releasing the canopy, I tried to go over the side but couldn't get free due to the centrifugal force. Finally, with a desperate lunge, I managed to get out but must have come in contact with the tail assembly because my face was scratched.

"Still in the overcast and free falling, I thought I had waited long enough, so I pulled the ripcord. The chute opened perfectly but I started to get lightheaded from lack of oxygen. After what seemed like an eternity, I broke out of the clouds and saw the ground rushing up at me. I guided the chute to avoid landing in a river and hit the ground with quite a jar.

"In about five seconds a Whermacht sergeant was on me with a Luger in my face. Needless to say, I surrendered. It developed that I had landed in a military installation, the artillery barracks at Celle, near Hanover.

"Nevertheless, I was glad to be on the ground and felt fine physically."

Two German guards took Williams and another American to Hanover and from there by train to Frankfurt.

"The city was a shambles from repeated bombings," Williams said, "as we left the station, a crowd began to gather. One woman called us English murderers, gangsters and accused us of killing her family in a raid (actually by the British) the night before. The guards convinced her we were Americans and not responsible.

A week of solitary confinement and two interrogations produced nothing more from Williams than his name, rank, and serial number. Shortly thereafter, he was among a group of prisoners who spent five days in boxcars en route to Stalagluft No. 1 at Barth in northern Germany, arriving there on Christmas Eve.

"We were stripped, deloused, and assigned to a barracks where twenty-six people lived in a small room. There were British and Russian prisoners along with Americans and for the next four months we kept up with the war news over a well-hidden radio.

"It was only a question of time and we knew approximately when to expect the Russian troops. On May 1st, I awoke to find the German guards had disappeared, and that day managed to get into the office and find my mug shot and German identity card. That night the Russians arrived.

"I was not physically mistreated during the confinement, but sure got to know a lot about hunger and cold. There was never enough food. I weighed 155 in late December and 115 when the camp was liberated."

His last mission had, in effect, lasted almost five months, placed a new meaning on the word survival, and prompted this thought from Williams: "You know the old saying about never volunteering for anything in the service."

MY BATTLE UP THE BOOT

by Richard A. Beranty

The U.S. Eighty-fifth Infantry Division was one of the Allied workhorses in Italy during World War II. Slugging its way up the Italian boot, the division faced some of the most formidable enemy positions devised in the European Theater of Operations, namely the Gustav Line near Minturno and the Gothic Line south of Bologna. The German soldiers manning these defenses were a determined and battle-tested lot, dug-in behind minefields and barbed-wire barricades with artillery and machine gun emplacements carved into rock or built from concrete. To engage this enemy, men of the Eighty-fifth had to contend with the Appenine Mountains, a chain of peaks and ridges that runs the length of Italy and reaches heights of over 5,000 feet. With few roads on the lower slopes and just goat trails on the upper reaches, mules were routinely used by the Americans to bring supplies in and take the wounded out. Add to those conditions the rainy months of fall and spring, and the frigid cold of a mountain winter, the battle for Italy was a grinding and bloody yard-by-yard fight that seemed to the common foot soldier to go on forever.

Long before its arrival in Italy the Eighty-fifth was dubbed the "Custer Division" from its World War I training days at Camp Custer near Battle Creek, Michigan. Its shoulder patch, a circle of khaki on which the monogram "CD" appears in red letters, reflects that history. Once home from the fields of France, the division was inactivated and remained so until America's entry into World War II when it was reorganized and its men began two years of stateside training. They arrived at Naples in March 1944, taking up positions along the Gustav Line near Minturno. Following the winter stalemate of 1943-44, Allied forces in May broke through the German defenses and their subsequent advance from the Anzio and Cassino areas had the enemy on the run. This breakout swept northward across the flat coastal regions south of Rome which was declared an open city in the wake of the fleeing Germans. On June 4th, Americans entered the Italian capital and a day later men of the Eighty-fifth took part in that city's liberation celebration. One of the division soldiers present was Paul R. McNelis, a twenty-year-old infantry replacement at that time, who as a member of the 338th Infantry Regiment, Second Battalion, Company E, went on to receive the Bronze Star (for valor) and the Purple Heart in fighting north of Rome. McNelis was one of the lucky ones, and this is his story.

Courtesy of Paul R. McNelis

Pictured stateside prior to being sent overseas, Paul R. McNelis of Kittanning, PA, went on to receive the Bronze Star Medal for Valor and Purple Heart in fighting north of Rome in 1944.

Born November 7, 1923, in Hastings, Cambria County, Pennsylvania, McNelis had three semesters of college under his belt before enlisting in the army on February 9, 1943, thus ending his college deferment.

"That's where everybody was going," McNelis says of his enlistment.

He arrived at Cumberland Gap on February 16th and was sent to Camp McCain in Grenada, Mississippi, where trainees lived in tar-paper shacks and faced no other alternative but to build wooden sidewalks and boardwalks around their quarters to get out of the mud. Just two weeks after his induction, however, McNelis contracted meningitis which left him at 121 pounds upon recovery. He was put into the newly formed Eighty-seventh Division following basic training and participated in winter maneuvers in Tennessee that gave generals, he says, practice at moving troops in battle and supplying an army in the field. Later that year, the division was moved to Fort Jackson, South Carolina, where McNelis was trained in infantry tactics as a squad leader and in the use of a BAR [Browning automatic rifle] and M-1 rifle.

"We were housed in barracks at Fort Jackson," McNelis says. "It was a fort, a permanent installation, versus a camp, which is temporary."

Because of casualties in overseas units, McNelis was taken out of the Eighty-seventh and sent to Africa aboard the U.S.S. General Mann on April 25, 1944. He arrived in Oran, Algeria, nine days later and remained there for about two weeks where he remembers the desert surroundings as quite inhospitable to the troops. He says soldiers used empty C-ration cans as coffee cups and frequently conducted business with the native inhabitants.

"We were issued mattress covers, which we sold to the Arabs," McNelis says. "They used them for a robe, cutting out arm holes and a neck hole. They made their Sunday suit out of them."

McNelis left Africa in a convoy of British ships bound for Naples. He was sent to a replenishment depot (called a "repple depple" in G.I. talk) at Caserta and assigned to a service company in the rear units of the Eighty-fifth.

"That's where I have my first recollection of war," McNelis says. "This grave registration outfit had American casualties, dead G.I.s, stacked up like cordwood. And they were black from decomposition. I was so damn dumb I thought they were all Negroes because the bodies were black."

McNelis remained with that service company throughout the Allied push from the Anzio-Cassino areas as the retreating Germans fled northward. In their advance toward Rome, McNelis says Americans encountered enemy rear-guard troops which tried to slow their pace. It was a tactic the Germans used again north of Rome as they fled toward the defensive fortifications of the Gothic Line.

"We went into Rome in single file, walking down both sides of the road," McNelis says. "A couple of days later, they had a big ceremony. Gen. Mark Clark (the U.S. Fifth Army ground commander) liked his flags flying and lots of photographers around. He was not thought of in great esteem by our soldiers. When he arrived in Rome, they had a big ceremony in front of the Victor Emanuel Palace. Secretary of War Henry L. Stimson presided. Rome was the first Axis capital to fall to Allied troops. After evacuating Rome, Field Marshal Alfred Kesselring, Germany's ablest defensive strategist, withdrew his two armies from the onrushing Allies. He hoped to inflict the maximum delay possible on their fast-charging pace by planting mines, exploding demolitions, and sacrificing his second-rate units in order to gain time and reach the Gothic Line defenses. If the Allied advance could be held up long enough, the good weather months would pass bringing the rain of September and October and the snow of November and December. The Allies would then be forced into another winter stalemate just as they were at Cassino the previous year.

"We were only in Rome for a very short time," McNelis explains. "The field units were chasing the Germans, who hadn't set up any prepared defenses except rear guard action to slow us. We chased them north of Rome about fifteen miles. My outfit came off the line and that's when I was introduced to Company E. From then on I was in combat."

By early August, Allied forces had reached Florence advancing some 270 miles in sixty-four days. McNelis says the first time he tasted real combat battle was west of Florence along the Arno River where the Eighty-fifth took over defense of the river's south bank on a front of about twenty-four miles. The Americans routinely sent out patrols to probe the enemy defenses and to take prisoners for interrogation as to German plans.

"We did a river crossing at a town called Empoli," he says. "We were scattered, dispersed along the river bank. Patrols were sent across at night. A few fire fights occurred but nothing major. At one point, battalion came up with this idea to set up permanent combat patrols. They wanted these people to do the main scouting, to stay ahead of the division. I said, 'Sure, I'll go.' Fortunately, they didn't take me. Those guys didn't last long."

The Eighty-fifth attacked the advance defenses of the Gothic

Line on September 13th. To division soldiers, the mountains in front of them concealing German positions looked like a solid wall of rock, the steepest portions of which were mostly on the southern, or attacking, side. On their lower slopes a wagon road generally wound its way to a farmhouse; beyond that, goat trails prevailed. At the highest elevations nothing existed but jagged rock. In all, these mountains afforded the German army ideal positions for defense with infantry dispersed in foxholes, behind rocks on dominating points, or inside of buildings. Its artillery guns and mortar crews were often out of reach, situated on the reverse sides of the mountains and zeroed in on areas from which U.S. troops might attack.

"The Germans were dug in, entrenched," McNelis offers. "It was tough warfare, similar to World War I type of fighting. The Germans were smart. They were depressed in the hills. Battles were constant. We'd go up one mountain, drive the enemy off or get knocked off ourselves. If we got our ass kicked off, our artillery would shell the mountain. We'd go back up, and what used to be a forest was just snags of trees. Then different groups, small patrols actually, would try to take the mountain peaks. They probed the enemy, trying to find a weak spot. Eventually, somebody would find a way in behind them, and the Germans would get word that we were going to flank them, so they would pull back to the next mountain. That's the kind of war it was.

"And they had excellent artillery," he continues. "Some were rocket-launched screaming meemies. From what I was told, the noise was created by loosening a little ring on the shell. They were frightening. You could hear them coming. They sounded like a truck coming in sideways. And even though Italy was not suited to tank warfare, you'd see some occasionally. Their tanks were equipped with 88 mm. guns and were very accurate. They would pull a tank to the brow of a hill, use it as artillery while we were trying to climb up. They they'd back off and the tank would be gone to another sector. Americans were constantly getting killed."

In its initial attack against the Gothic Line, two mountain passes faced the Eighty-fifth. One was Futa Pass, heavily defended with concrete bunkers and minefields. The other was Il Giogo Pass, less defended but narrower and steeper. General Clark opted to attack through the latter, and committed three divisions to the battle. In five days of fighting the Gothic Line was breached. Although the

Germans had no official line of prepared defenses to fall back on before the Po Valley, forty miles of mountainous terrain still remained. It was simply a continuation of the Gothic Line to Allied soldiers. At this time, McNelis was made an acting squad leader in charge of fifteen men despite retaining his Pfc. rating.

"After some amount of combat, you lose a lot of squad leaders," McNelis explains. "They're among the first ones you lose. So they made me an acting squad leader. I was running a squad as a Pfc. for several months. The reason being, they started disbanding units like Ack-Ack, air control people who came in with ratings, sergeants and above. In the table of organization, there just wasn't room for that many sergeants. So I stayed a Pfc. until some time later."

Following the battle for Il Giogo pass, the next objective for McNelis' regiment was Firenzuola, six miles to the north. It was the last town of any size in the division's sector south of the Po River. The town was captured on September 21st and the next day McNelis says his company was held up by heavy machine gun fire from the crest of Hill 733 near Poggio, a mountain village about two miles northeast of Firenzuola. In the ensuing fight, McNelis' platoon leader, 1st Lt. Orville E. Bloch, earned the Medal of Honor for eliminating five machine gun nests single handedly.

"I was with him along with three other guys," McNelis says. "We had had a tough battle earlier, taking this mountain ridge. I mean it was a tough battle. Eventually we overcame them and had taken some prisoners, about fifty. Lieutenant Bloch asked me and another guy to take these prisoners back, turn them over to MPs. When I got back up to the line, I asked where Bloch was. 'He went to that village up there,' somebody said. I thought it best to report in, so I headed up to find him. It was like climbing alongside a big cliff with one narrow passageway to the village. When I got there, hell, I didn't know what was going on, but he had already charged one machine gun nest.

"So Bloch grabbed me," McNelis continues, "and told me to cover a street corner. There were only about three houses there, but they were all connected. I took the corner, looked up the street and saw Germans. I fired at them, and they ducked into some doorways. I went into one, and there was a German soldier, a kid who probably wasn't any more than fifteen years old, lying on a table. His stomach looked like somebody took a knife and cut him all the way across. He was lying there trying to hold his stomach together.

"We carried morphine inside our helmet, just a little tube of it, and I gave him a shot. After that, I had to get out of there. Things were hot. We went back down the hill, because our line was on this ridge behind us, and we were out in front of it, vulnerable. We weren't sure where the remaining Germans were."

Following the action in and around Firenzuola, the Eighty-fifth moved forward over increasingly rugged mountains. The last great ridge of the Appenines had been conquered by the end of September, but twenty miles still remained to reach the Po Valley. Rain began falling on September 20th and continued for the next week. Heavy rains started on September 29th and lasted until October 9th. Area streams became raging rivers as water poured off the barren hillsides. Roads, trails, and bridges were washed out. Allied air support was grounded and lines of communications were downed. Artillery had to be towed into position by bulldozer and the troops, by and large, suffered physically and psychologically from the conditions. As he had hoped, Kesselring was winning the race with the weather.

"You can't live out in the open forever," McNelis says. "You have to have shelter. We are human beings, and can only take so much or nobody is worth anything. So whenever we found a farmhouse, a barn, or a cowshed, we got inside of it. And remember, this is high up in the Appenines. The spine of Italy are these mountains. But generally speaking, we weren't on the line for any more than fifteen consecutive days depending on the situation, or three weeks at the very most, before they pulled us back to the rear slope of a mountain, let us rest for about a day and brought up the hot food. A cook would be sent up for each squad or platoon. They would set up in a barn and warm up these ten-in-one rations.

"Otherwise, on the line we survived on K-rations," he explains. "Mules brought them up at night along with ammunition and water. K-rations were in boxes about the size of a Cracker Jack box. Breakfast was a little can of ham and eggs, three crackers, four cigarettes, and instant coffee. Lunch was the same thing, plus lemonade powder. Instead of the eggs, though, we got a can of cheese loaf. For supper, there was a can of beef and pork loaf in them. We were happy to get that stuff. C-rations, of course, were better. They had more of a variety, like ham and beans. But we didn't get any of them since they were bulkier and we were being supplied by mules. If you were on the line K-rations weren't that bad. One good thing about them was that the box was impregnated with wax. There was just enough that when you set it on fire it would warm a cup of coffee. A buddy of mine, David Milton, was the first one who showed me how to make toasted cheese. You open the can, stick your bayonet in it and hold it over that fire to melt the cheese and then put it on the crackers. But you had to be careful about lighting fires. You didn't want to bring enemy fire on you.

"There were also times when we came across a farmhouse," he continues. "They all contained a barrel of wine, so we did have some wine to drink. Occasionally we also found a civilian inside. I guess they decided to stay and hope the war would pass them by. They were generally friendly; we didn't force anything on them. But if there were chickens around, somebody would steal them. And in some places, we would swap the meat out of our K-rations for eggs. That would be a one-time exchange. They wouldn't give us any more eggs after that. They had no taste for our K-rations."

If obtaining food was a tough challenge, staying clean, dry, and warm was even more difficult.

"When we came off the line, sometimes they would set up shower units along a river, about once every three or four weeks," McNelis explains. "Here we could exchange our clothes for some that they boiled from the previous group. These units were pretty efficient in that they took everything we wore and gave us back a fresh uniform. It didn't necessarily fit, but it was nice because it was clean."

On October 10th, the 338th Regiment reached positions from which it began an attack on Mount Della Formiche, a series of steep cliffs which was important to the German defenders because of its commanding view of Highway 65. Two villages at the foot of the mountain were cleared of the enemy after a day of heavy fighting.

"We were on the approaches to Mount Formiche," McNelis says. "It was pretty open area. They asked me to take a patrol, six guys, up this hill which our artillery had just pasted. So we're going up in this ditch area, trying to stay concealed and covered because it was daytime. We didn't catch any fire, but when we got further up, we saw a cluster of farmhouses, about three or four buildings, in front of a cliff. We got up to it, went across the patio going into this farmhouse, and I heard a noise down in the cellar. I hollered, 'Quando Tadeski,' meaning, 'How many Germans' in Italian. Damn if one didn't come up. So I somehow said, 'Anymore down there?' He said, 'Quanti?' I said, 'Yeah.' I think he said four. 'Andante,' I told him, meaning, 'Get them up here.' Believe it or not, they started coming out. We had ten or twelve Germans come up from this basement, and we only had a patrol. So we were pretty anxious to get rid of them. But by then, the guys behind us started to arrive.

"So we consolidated our positions late in the afternoon, getting everybody up from the valley. We had some guys in a little outbuilding alongside the houses and some in foxholes as security. After dark, the Germans counterattacked, came down and caught the guys in this outbuilding firing into it with what we called 'beehives.' They were like bazookas. The Germans killed a bunch of our guys. We probably lost more there in a period of an hour than in any other battle."

A day later, in another fight for one of the hills on Mount Formiche, McNelis' actions won him the Bronze Star for valor. His citation, dated October 12th, for heroic achievement in action in the vicinity of Carpenaccia, on Hill 754 due east of Peglio, reads as follows:

> While reconnoitering for possible enemy positions and beyond the requirements of his mission, Pfc. McNelis, squad leader, noticed a battery of enemy mortars. Without regard for his personal safety, he crept forward silently and investigated while the other members of his squad kept his advance covered. He took three enemy prisoners and destroyed the mortars returning the prisoners to the company. He reported definite and accurate information that there were no more enemy to our front. His heroic action secured the entire hill.

"Medals are generally given because of where you happen to be, who saw it, and who writes you up," McNelis says. "I can tell you about a lot of other times when we should have had some medals, but didn't get any. But in this instance, we had just taken a ridge and we were consolidating and it was hot. My squad was out of water. So I got this guy named John McAleavey and said to him, 'John, let's take the canteens and go to that farmhouse down there and get some water.' I figured there had to be a well somewhere. So I'm carrying these canteens armed with a P-38 pistol which I had taken from a German casualty earlier. I usually didn't take anything from dead or captured Germans because we were in combat. You don't want to have any of their stuff on you if you're captured because they'd probably kill you for having their equipment.

"But it was nice to have a pistol as a sidearm. McAleavey was a BAR man at the time and we headed for this farmhouse. Like most of them it was built on the back slope of a hill. From one entryway you go straight into the upstairs, or the main floor. Then down behind there usually was a kitchen. A lot of times the Italians kept their animals in there for heat to warm the house. Somehow, my buddy and I separated. I went into the upper area, straight in, and there were some German packs lying there. So I started to look around and all at once I heard shooting. I scooted outside and came back around the farmhouse, and there's Mac shooting in the windows like a cowboy. He had these guys captured in the kitchen area. So I started firing the pistol and they came out, surrendered, and as the citation says they were part of a mortar set-up who weren't normally on the front lines. Usually they were behind the line like artillery. Mt. Della Formiche was quite a battle."

The taking of Formiche threw large numbers of the enemy into confusion and many surrendered. In nearly a month and a half since its attack on the Gothic Line, the division captured 2,000 prisoners. The 338th Regiment gradually moved through more rough country toward Mount Fano, which it captured on October 20th. The Germans continued with their delaying tactics and every night American patrols were sent out to try and make contact with them. Toward the end of October, the regiment was poised to attack the strong points of Pizzano and Orbega to the northwest which were the last dominating mountains south of the Po Valley now only eight miles away. On October 25th, McNelis had part of his leg blown apart by an enemy grenade. His memories of that day and subsequent recovery remain vivid.

"For a change we were going downhill," McNelis relates. "We had our command post in this barn and set up foxholes around the perimeter, security for that night. They asked me to take a patrol to see if the Germans had pulled out. So we started down, this was about eleven o'clock at night, and it was dark. Our platoon sergeant, a guy by the name of Jackson, came up from behind me and asked, 'Where are our lines?' I said, 'See that rock cliff up there? Don't get out in front of it because that's our line.' Well, we went about twenty yards ahead and, 'Bang!' He somehow had gotten out in front of our so-called lines and one of our guys killed him. We went back to the command post and found out what had happened. Then we continued again with the patrol.

"Now it's black night," he continues. "We went back down to the same general area, threw grenades, yelled, hollered, shot. We got nothing in return so we assumed the Germans were gone and we went back to the command post where we found guys from another outfit. Their unit had tried earlier to get into this same town and got kicked back so they sent some people up to us to lead in from our positions. Since we had been down there, David Milton and I left with this patrol. Now it's four o'clock in the morning. It's so black you can't see your hand. We went down a little further than where we had been earlier and saw a haystack, about twenty-feet high. Milton asked, 'What are we going to do?' I said, 'You go around this side and I'll go around the other side.' So we did, and we're standing behind this haystack and Milton said, 'There's a foxhole over there.'

"He was right. For protection, a German had dug his foxhole behind this haystack. And I felt that the Germans had withdrawn so I took my M-1 and kind of probed inside the hole and said, 'They're gone, see. There's nobody in there.' As soon as I said that a German came out firing a zip gun. He must have had a telephone line laid into his hole because when I turned around, instinctively pulling my trigger, I tripped over something. By then the shots had alerted everyone around there and apparently another German hole was close by and somebody threw a grenade."

McNelis says his bullets hit the German soldier at point-blank range.

"He was moaning, trying to get out of the foxhole, and I grabbed hold of him," he explains. "Can you believe it? I'm going to pull this German out of his foxhole! Why? I don't know. You just do things, and it all happened so damn fast. I didn't know what happened with Milton. I thought he was killed by that zip gun, but as I found out just recently he wasn't killed. He was taken prisoner and later died of wounds in captivity. So the grenade landed right behind me, exploded and I dropped the German and ran around the corner on the up-slope behind the haystack. I didn't realize that I was hit until I felt blood running down my leg. Then I thought, 'Man, I got to do something!'

"Fortunately I saw two helmets, silhouettes in the sky, and I hollered at these two guys who were with this outfit that had been trying to get in there earlier. They came over and I put an arm over each of their shoulders and they hauled me back to our command post. We had a medic assigned to us and he dressed up the wound. I don't think it was a fragmentation grenade, a German potato masher, because it has a sleeve of metal to launch fragments in all directions. I had a lot of tin up my leg, plus this blowout on my calf, so I think it was a concussion grenade. If it had been a potato masher, I doubt if I would have survived because it exploded right behind me. So the command post called battalion, which had medics, stretcher bearers, and they came down from the battalion aid station, about a mile or two behind us, and carried me back."

McNelis says the next morning, he was placed on a stretcher and across a jeep which took him to the edge of a mountain ridge. He was then thrown over a mule which carried him off the mountain to a river bottom where an ambulance waited. He was driven to an aid station near Florence and transferred to a hospital near Leghorn on the west coast of Italy where doctors operated.

"We were lined up on stretchers," McNelis relates, "waiting to be operated on. Those doctors worked a lot of overtime. I don't know how long the lines were, but they were long. Before I went in for the operation I must have been asleep because I woke up and the guy next to me was looking at this Purple Heart. I said, 'Where did you get that?' He said, 'You got one.' So I looked down and there was one on my stretcher. They took me in, patched me up and did a lot of stitching. I was in Leghorn for maybe a week before they decided that I should be in a hospital further back, so we went by hospital boat from Leghorn to Naples."

Four days after being wounded, McNelis wrote a letter to his parents. Dated October 29th, its optimistic tone indicates a desire to spare his parents news of the seriousness of his wounds. It reads as follows:

Dear Mom and Dad,

I thought it best to write as soon as possible and let you know that I have been wounded slightly. I hope this reaches you before the official telegram comes so that you will not be worried too much, and that I am alright.

It was about four o'clock in the morning of the 25th that I was hit a couple places in the right leg by fragments from a hand grenade, but I was able to get back to our lines with help.

I'm in the Sixty-fourth General Hospital and will probably be here for awhile. The food is swell; we have sheets and pajamas, and I expect to be walking around in a day or so.

Again I ask you not to worry. I really haven't had much pain. I'll be able to write pretty often now so you can expect to hear from me as I am expecting to hear from you.

Your son,
Paul

Courtesy of Paul R. McNelis

Enjoying a respite from the front lines in March, 1945, McNelis (on the left) is pictured in Rome with two fellow GIs.

"Our recuperation tents were in a tangerine grove near Caserta," he says. "It was nice, really. We ate tangerines until we got sick. I think I stayed in Naples for so long because the doctors wanted to see if they could salvage the skin and muscle from deteriorating around this blast on my calf. They kept wet bandages on it, trying to keep it moist enough to get a skin graft going. Eventually it dried up; they couldn't save it. So one day a doctor came in and said to me and the guy next to me, 'You two are lucky. You're both going home.' I thought, 'I'll believe that when I see it.' Well, I didn't see it. Every Friday, a panel of doctors examined the men who they thought were ready to go back to the front. So on Thursday nights, guys would take a wet, knotted towel and beat on their wounds with it to try and get them redder and rawer. They hoped it would keep them away from the line one more week. Instead of using a towel, I would buckle my combat boot real tight over one of the wounds in my ankle area and walk around to make it red and raw in order to influence the doctors. It worked until I was sent up one Friday and they said, 'He looks pretty good. We'll send him back.' Before I knew it, I was back at the repple depple in Caserta and reassigned to the same outfit."

McNelis says he returned to the mud and snow of the front line in late February, this time as a sergeant. A lot of the men he knew were gone but some were still there. His company was positioned on a ridge overlooking Bologna and duty consisted of manning observation foxholes, sending out nightly patrols, and encountering German patrols as well.

"We had a foxhole which unfortunately was out in front of some barbed wire," McNelis says. "This one day was very foggy, we couldn't see very far, and the Germans came up and laid in wait at this foxhole which was to be manned by our troops. I guess they knew how much we stuck to schedule, because the Germans let two of our guys through the barbed wire, fired on and killed two others and took the first two captive. The next day I manned that foxhole, and the Germans had left a couple of their potato mashers in there. Well, things got boring, so I stuck them out in the snow in front of me and used them for target practice, to see if I could hit them, which I did."

By early April, the Allied armies were rested, reorganized, and re-equipped. Artillery ammunition was stockpiled as were supplies of gasoline and weapons and the ground offensive toward the Po Valley was launched. With the help of Allied air forces, enemy lines were quickly penetrated trapping German troops on the southern side of the Po River because the bridges crossing it were destroyed from the air. With little or no bridging equipment, thousands of Germans surrendered. Major enemy resistance ended by April 25th. Gen. Heinrich von Vietinghoff, who replaced Kesselring after he was called back to Germany to try his hand at delaying the Allied offensive in Western Europe, agreed to unconditional surrender of his army group effective at noon on May 2nd.

"When we finally broke through into the Po Valley from the Appenines, it was a rout," McNelis says. "The Germans had no way to defend once we broke their line in the mountains. They could have defended their next natural defensive position, which was the Po River, but they were so disorganized trying to get the hell back to Germany that they were in a rout. We were more or less chasing them. Occasionally, they set up holding actions, trying to delay us for maybe half a day until we took them out. Eventually we got up toward the vicinity of Verona and found the bridges across the river were blown. But there was one bridge that our air forces didn't do a very good job on. The rails across it were still kind of hanging, and we could walk along it. That's how we crossed that river. Then we started toward the Brenner Pass, which connects Italy with Austria, and we went up there maybe fifteen or twenty miles not hitting any opposition. Finally, our outfit was taken off the line and we went back to Verona where division headquarters was located. They always used a line outfit for security, so our company was assigned to secure division. That's where we were when the war ended.

GUSTAV LINE

With Sicily already fallen, Allied troops began the push up the Italian peninsula on September 3, 1943. By September 18th, southern Italy was liberated. German troops withdrew to the Gustav line. By November the Allied advance was completely stalled in front of it.

Learning from the lesson of the Maginot Line, the Gustav defenses cut across the entire peninsula. There were no gaps to slip through or flanks to turn. The rugged mountainous terrain was a natural fortification by itself. German military engineers added interlocking fire fields, strong concrete points, and hardened artillery emplacements. Thousands of Anglo-American troops died on its approaches.

The landing at Anzio was designed to place Allied troops in back of the Gustav line. German defenders pinned the invaders to the beach for three months before combined attacks fragmented German strength and a breakout at Anzio and a breakthrough on the Gustav line succeeded. This opened the road to Rome, which fell to the advancing Allies on June 7, 1944; the day after the Normandy Invasion had begun.

"I CROSSED THE RAPIDO"

By Richard A. Beranty

The attempted crossing of the Rapido River in Italy by two
infantry regiments of the U.S. Thirty-sixth Division in
January, 1944, was one of the costliest failed attacks made by
American forces during World War II. Nearly 2,000 men were
either killed, wounded, or captured in this so-called "Battle of Guts"
in the Liri Valley, a frontal assault aimed at breaking through the
vaunted Gustav Line near Cassino. What started as a diversionary
tactic to relieve pressure from the soon-to-be Anzio beachhead,
ended as an unforgettable and monstrous blood bath that achieved
nothing for the Allies in strategic gains.

"Everyone was very, very leery about the attack because we all felt
sure that it was going to be difficult," says James D. White of
Kittanning, Pennsylvania, at the time a nineteen-year-old infantry
replacement with the "Texas" division when the order came to cross
the icy-cold and rain-swollen Rapido. "But you do what you're told."

It wasn't the attack itself that sent waves of pessimism through
the ranks of division troops but rather where the attack took place.
Ordered to cross the Rapido at a dangerous S bend in the river, the
two regiments faced one of the most savagely defended streams in all
of Europe where every foot of ground, it seemed, was manned by
German forces. Murderous fire from rockets, artillery, mortars and
machine guns, emplaced behind miles of barbed wire and thousands
of mines, thwarted two attempted crossings and mauled the hapless
"T-patchers" while they struggled to reach the Rapido, fought to
cross it, and tried to establish a bridgehead on the other side.

"I went across on a little narrow footbridge, about two-feet wide,
which engineers had anchored to the other side," White explains.
"We didn't have that far to go so our whole battalion made it.
We no more had gotten across when the Germans opened up on us.

And did they ever! The terrain on that side of the river was flat so we started digging in right away, and for good reason. All morning and all day long the Germans poured artillery fire on us. Guys were getting square hit with mortar shells coming right into their foxholes. My first sergeant was hit with machine gun fire across his legs. Somebody got him dug into a hole and he took a square hit from a mortar. Because we were dug in so close together, the Germans couldn't miss us. Guys were being killed all around me."

The indiscriminate slaughter of men continued unabated throughout the day. There was no way for those stranded on the far side of the Rapido to receive supplies or re-cross the river and reach the safety of U.S. lines. German artillery crews saw to that by destroying their footbridges. Faced with no other option but to fight against overwhelming odds, the T-patchers held their ground until ammunition ran out and the relentless enemy fire overpowered them. White escaped death because he was taken prisoner and spent the rest of the war in a German POW camp. Many others, though, weren't so lucky. When division casualties were assessed after the attack, there was some question as to whether the Thirty-sixth could even continue as a fighting unit due to the appalling losses. Back home after the war, division veterans, men who had known combat and the lethal consequences that go with it, were still so incensed over what they felt was a needless sacrifice of human life kept a promise they made to each other years before and thousands of miles away. They petitioned Congress to investigate the Rapido-crossing fiasco and take the necessary steps to keep Gen. Mark W. Clark, U.S. Fifth Army commander in Italy at the time, from ever commanding troops in the field again. Their efforts failed and Clark was exonerated. But the memories of that cold January day, of dying men and the punishing German guns, have haunted Jim White ever since.

"I do feel a little bit guilty about surviving," he admits. "How did I make it back when all those other guys around me didn't? And I'm sure they had parents at home praying for them, the same as my mother and dad were praying for me. How did guys as close to me as five-feet away get hit and I didn't?"

White's journey across the Rapido began on May 12, 1943, when he was drafted and sent to the Infantry Replacement Training Center (IRTC) at Fort McClellan, Alabama, for seventeen weeks of basic training. He boarded a Liberty ship at Newport News, Virginia, on

November 3rd, and reached Oran, Algeria, twenty-one days later.

"From Oran we shipped over to Naples in early December on an LST. From there we went into a replenishment depot. We knew we were going to replace somebody in the infantry."

The urgent need for replacements was a constant for the Thirty-sixth in the early days of the Italian campaign. Since its invasion at Salerno three months earlier, the division had endured hard and continuous fighting on or near the coast that depleted its ranks considerably. Four days were needed to clear the Salerno beaches. Fighting in the hills above the Italian seaport grew even more intense. At Altavilla, Cpl. Charles E. "Commando" Kelly of Pittsburgh, America's first Medal of Honor winner in Europe, held off a bruising enemy attack alone by lobbing mortar shells as grenades from a second-story balcony because he was out of ammunition. At Monte Rotondo and Monte Lungo, the division was under fire for twenty-four consecutive days and nights. And in battles around San Pietro, it suffered 2,400 casualties. This was fighting, however, that many in the division hadn't anticipated. One day prior to their September 9 landing, news was announced of Italy's unconditional surrender to the Allies and optimism soared among the troops still on ships off the Italian coast. They thought the liberation of Italy would be an easy ride. Taking the country might last a month; two at the most. Their hopes, however, were short-lived. Overlooked was the fact that German troops still garrisoned the country and reinforcements were on the way. This so-called "cake-walk" would see some of the bitterest fighting in the ETO against a very stubborn, well-led and well-equipped enemy. With so many new faces arriving to fill the empty slots, the T on the shoulder patches of division soldiers now stood for just about anywhere.

"Most of the men were originally from Texas, close to the majority were," says White. "But with so many casualties they were pretty depleted when we went in. When I joined up with them, the division had recently been pulled off the line. It was on break. As soon as we replacements arrived, the division moved up to the front."

It had been raining when White joined the Thirty-sixth, first assigned to a rifle company and then later to a 60 mm. mortar squad in Third Battalion, Company K of the 141st Regiment. Day after day of cold winter rain left much of the countryside an endless expanse of mud. Foxholes, normally a ground soldier's only refuge on the battlefield, were filled with water. Trench foot, which occurs when tissues of the feet die from exposure to wetness, was common. White says that life on the line was one of constant movement, poor food, wet clothes, and cold feet.

"You're in a foxhole for awhile, then you move up," he says. "You might spend one or two nights in the same place, then move forward. It was raining all the time, and it was cold. My feet were frozen. Most of the guys had frozen feet. They told us not to take our boots off because we never knew when we might have to get out of somewhere in a hurry. And if you did take your boots off you might not be able to get them back on because your feet would swell up."

By mid-January the Thirty-sixth was positioned on the west side of the Rapido River along the Gustav Line with the crest of Monte Cassino and the ancient Benedictine abbey atop it looming in the distance. The gloom that most division soldiers felt about any upcoming assault was shared by Gen. Fred L. Walker, commanding general of the Thirty-sixth, who at the time pleaded with Clark to reconsider the attack saying: "It is always wise to strike the enemy where he is weakest." Walker knew the Germans were not weak, but he had another reason to feel pessimistic. The Thirty-sixth at that time was not a top-notch fighting outfit. It had been battered at Salerno and beyond, and many of its officers were new and not yet acquainted with the men.

"A company commander didn't last long," White offers. "General Walker was definitely against the crossing but he was following orders from above."

On the enemy's side of the river, troops were commanded by Field Marshal Alfred Kesselring, a defense-minded German general who previously headed Axis forces in Sicily. Kesselring knew the Americans were readying an attack because U.S. patrols had crossed the river several days beforehand and the resulting skirmishes alerted the Germans who then doubled their efforts in fortifying the low terrain by stringing more barbed wire and cutting away trees that hindered the field of fire. In Clark's mind a daylight crossing was out of the question and he ordered it to take place at night. To help relieve some of the pressure, a massive Allied build-up just off the western coast of Italy was ready to put troops ashore at Anzio and Nettuno beaches which planners hoped would draw German forces away from Cassino and break the winter stalemate there. If that scenario didn't play out, the attack across the Rapido would hopefully draw German troops away from the Anzio area so that invasion would succeed. Neither outcome materialized, however, because of the lethargic movement of the Allies to break out of the Anzio beachhead allowing Kesselring to hold off his enemies on both fronts by moving troops freely between the two areas.

The battle plan at Cassino called for French forces to initially cross the Rapido and take the hills to the north while the British attacked on the south. The Thirty-sixth was then to deliver the main assault in the center. After the T-patchers established a bridgehead, Clark envisioned the U.S. First Armored Division crossing the river, going through the Thirty-sixth and speeding north toward Anzio and eventually Rome.

"I don't see how they could have possibly gotten tanks, let alone bridges, across that river," White says. "We could look out and see it before we crossed. It's called a river, but I would call it a stream. Where I crossed it was no more than fifteen- to twenty-feet wide. But it was a real fast moving stream. It was a mountain stream; deep and very swift."

On January 12th, French forces made up of Moroccans and Algerians began the attack on the right. After four days of close fighting, some of which included the use of bayonets, the French Expeditionary Corps was halted and pulled back. The British assault didn't fare much better. Two of its divisions attacked on the left on January 17th. Kesselring was fearful this force would breach his line, so he pulled two divisions away from the Anzio sector and the fighting ended in a stalemate. So without flank protection, Clark gave orders for the Thirty-sixth to attack just south of Cassino on the night of January 20th. To soften up German defenses, fourteen battalions of Allied artillery bombarded their positions but it wasn't enough to give the foot soldiers a chance at success. The division's 141st and 143rd regiments began the crossing with the 142nd in reserve. Troops crossed over in wooden boats and rubber rafts or on footbridges under terrific enemy fire.

"We tried crossing at about two in the morning," White says. "The first night we tried, we didn't make it. We got pushed back. The engineers were to have cleared the minefield going down to the river. We were to follow strips of tape, white reflective tape that we could see at night. My squad leader was up ahead of us and I don't know whether he stepped over the tape or the engineers missed a mine. I don't know what it was. But anyhow he tramped on a mine and it blew his leg off just below the knee. He was conscious, though, and a couple of guys put a tourniquet on it."

To hamper any attempted crossing, the Germans had released water from power dams upstream just days before which made the flood plain on the U.S. side a quagmire of marshes. The muddy ground prevented trucks from supporting the attack so troops had to carry assault boats and cables to the river. For about two miles soldiers lugged these bulky twenty-four-man rubber rafts and twelve-man wooden assault boats to their crossing sites, the latter measuring thirteen-feet long and weighing more than 400 pounds. Troops started to encounter German shells about a mile from the Rapido and chaos reigned in the winter darkness. One company had its commander killed, its second-in-command wounded, and 30 enlisted men lost in a single volley. Explosions punctured the rubber boats and splintered the wooden ones. Tape indicating the way was torn up and buried in the mud. When the 141st finally made it to the river, about one-third of the boats couldn't be used. Troops laden down with weapons and ammunition tried to board the boats swinging crazily in the treacherous current. While some craft got across, some were hit by artillery fire, some capsized, and some were swept downstream. Of the four footbridges, all were destroyed although engineers managed to re-erect one. Two companies crossed that lone footbridge until it, too, was destroyed. By 10:00 A.M. this first attack was called off as the guns of those who had crossed grew silent. White says he carried a mortar slung over his right shoulder during the assault and a .30 caliber carbine positioned horizontally across both shoulders.

"We were getting shelled, so of course I hit the dirt two or three times," he says. "Every time I did I always reached back to make sure my gun was still there. One time I reached back and my gun was gone. I didn't know where it was. I thought, 'Oh, man! What am I going to do now?' So we got back to our positions and I told my squad leader, 'I lost my carbine.' One of the guys in my squad was carrying a .45, and he had to go back to the medics. He was sick. So he said, 'I'll leave you my .45.' Well, I had never fired a .45 before. I didn't know much about a .45, but I thought it was better than nothing. So I took it."

White also lost his glasses in the action.

"I've always worn glasses," he continues. "When we were getting shelled, I hit the dirt and the concussion knocked my helmet off and pulled my glasses off at the same time. It was dark, and I was feeling around, trying to find them, and the company was moving on. So I picked up my helmet and kept on going. I didn't have glasses until I returned to the states."

Ordered back to their previous positions following the failed crossing, morale among the T-patchers was even lower than it had been before. Men cursed and prayed that the assault would be canceled.

"Boy, we were hoping that they would change the plan," White says. "We thought surely they wouldn't try it again."

But they did. On the following night, January 21st, the same two regiments were again ordered to cross the river.

"On the second try we came down more or less the same path," he says. "But, there was no enemy fire. Everything was quiet. The Germans just let us come down."

White says the German strategy of allowing the early units to cross the river unmolested and then letting loose with everything they had worked to perfection. First the footbridges were destroyed. Then the boats, still full of men and still coming over, were targeted. That accomplished, German guns went to work on the stranded GIs. At that time dawn had started to break and White was one of those facing this methodical destruction. It included the use of the eight-barreled rockets dubbed Screaming Meemies because of their distinctive and terrifying sound.

"You could hear them coming. They go, 'whrill, whrill, whrill.' The sound alone scares you as much as anything."

No support arrived for the T-patchers as the day wore on. A third attack to include the 142nd Regiment (still in reserve) was canceled only after Walker complained to Clark. But the men on the east side of the river were still holding out and still taking a pounding. By afternoon the Germans launched a series of counterattacks that were beaten back by the hard-pressed Americans. The enemy's withdrawal was followed by intense German artillery fire that zeroed in on the areas marked by their previous attacks. Those T-patchers still alive were dug in and hunkered down trying to offer as much resistance as they could while facing withering fire from the Germans.

"We held out that first day," White says. "We got some Germans. They didn't get us that first day. So the next morning several of us, the ones who were able, got back down to the bridge where we had crossed. Here, the Germans hit the bridge, a square hit, and it was knocked out. We were trying to figure out how to get back across the river, when a fellow with us said, 'I'll try to swim it. If I get a rope across maybe we can get back.' So we put a rope around him and he tried to swim. But he couldn't. The current carried him downstream. We pulled him back in and it was just breaking daylight. This would have been on the 23rd of January and the Germans saw us. I think they thought everybody had been wiped out the previous day and as soon as they saw us they opened up again."

With the Thirty-sixth now just a shell of its former fighting self, Gen. Geoffrey Keyes, the II Corps commander, stopped the attack forty-eight hours after it started. Without making a dent in the German line, the division suffered 1,976 casualties: 136 officers and men killed, 932 wounded, and 908 missing. White was taken prisoner about 100 yards from the river with about twenty-five to fifty others. He was searched, was allowed to keep his dogtags and Bible, but did have his field jacket taken from him.

"The Germans wanted that for themselves to keep warm," he says.

The captured T-patchers then feared for the worst.

"We didn't know what was going to happen. We thought they might shoot us because they took us down over a hill and I thought, 'My God, this is it!' But all they wanted us to do was gather some dead German soldiers and bring their bodies back. So we did that. Then they started moving us behind the lines until we got back to another area, like a small prison camp. We were there for a couple of days and lived in tents. It was cold."

Their days as frontline soldiers now over, the men were crowded into boxcars on a train bound for Germany and fourteen months of imprisonment. White says he isn't sure how long the train ride lasted.

"You lose track of time," he says. " You're in there, locked in and shut in. We couldn't see out and we didn't get fed, so I lost track of time. I would guess two or three days, but I couldn't say for sure. Inside the boxcar we were right up against each other, standing up the whole time. There was no room to hardly even move. And my feet were frozen so badly I couldn't stand anybody touching them. To relieve ourselves, there was a little keg in the middle of the car with only enough room for one person. Once somebody got on there, we had to wait."

The train's first stop was at a German camp housing British prisoners where it remained for about two days.

"The British tried to help us as much as they could. I do remember that they gave me a British army jacket to replace the one taken from me."

The men were then moved to permanent quarters, Stalag II B in northeastern Germany near the town of Hammerstein in eastern Prussia, where they were housed with other privates, corporals, and sergeants in long barracks ringed by fences, barbed wire, gun towers, and ever-present guards. White estimates there were about 2,000 prisoners in the main camp, some of whom were also from the Thirty-sixth.

"There were guys there from the division, but none from my company. Not too many of *them* were left."

The German troops in charge of the camp did not feel compelled to supply the men with a decent meal. White says they were fed once a day in the evening.

"For food they gave us some kind of weak soup and a loaf of bread. That had to be divided between seven guys," he says. "We would measure it up exactly because it meant so much. I know the bread was made of sawdust because you could see the sawdust in it. It was black after being baked. You could tell it was sawdust."

Prisoners were sent on work parties not long after their arrival and lived away from the main camp in smaller, barbed-wire enclosed compounds, housed in a building with bars on the windows. Some worked on nearby potato farms; White cut timber in a forest with nineteen other men. To supplement their meager rations, Red Cross parcels started to arrive which contained cans of Spam or corned beef, biscuits, soap, razors, toilet tissue, and cigarettes.

"Getting Red Cross parcels was the only thing that kept us going," he says. "We were supposed to get one a week, but we didn't always get them once a week."

Baths were just as uncommon an occurrence.

"When I was first captured, I went several weeks without a shave or a shower. The first time in the main POW camp we were given a cold shower. In the work camp we eventually were given a tub and we heated water and bathed once a week."

Back home in western Pennsylvania, White's parents received what every parent with sons in the service dreaded at the time: a Western Union telegram. It is dated March 13, 1944, and is contained today in a scrapbook that his mother put together. It reads as follows:

THE SECRETARY OF WAR DESIRES ME TO EXPRESS HIS DEEPEST REGRET THAT YOUR SON PRIVATE JAMES D. WHITE HAS BEEN REPORTED MISSING IN ACTION SINCE 23 JAN

> IN ITALY PERIOD IF FURTHER DETAILS OR
> OTHER INFORMATION ARE RECEIVED YOU
> WILL BE PROPERLY NOTIFIED

"I guess it was pretty hard on my mom," White says. "Her health wasn't too good to begin with and I was an only child."

A second telegram, dated April 14, 1944, arrived at his parents' home with somewhat better news.

> BASED ON INFORMATION RECEIVED
> THROUGH THE PROVOST MARSHAL GENERAL
> RECORDS OF THE WAR DEPARTMENT HAVE
> BEEN AMENDED TO SHOW YOUR SON PRIVATE
> JAMES D. WHITE IS NOW A PRISONER OF WAR
> OF THE GERMAN GOVERNMENT PERIOD ANY
> FURTHER INFORMATION WILL BE FURNISHED
> BY THE PROVOST MARSHAL GENERAL

"That telegram relieved my mom considerably," he says. "At least she knew that I was alive."

With his POW address in their possession, White's parents began sending letters, food packages, and cigarettes to their son. Several order receipts for Camels, mailed to servicemen at the time by the R.J. Reynolds Tobacco Company, are contained in White's scrapbook. One is dated August 14, 1944. The cost of the order was $1.41.

"My parents knew I didn't smoke, but they thought I could use them to barter," he says. "Once in a while you might find a German guard who was willing to trade. We always said to them: 'Havensee brot for kaufen?' That meant, 'Do you have any bread for trading?' Most of them smoked and some of them were willing to trade."

Health care for the prisoners, at least that provided by the Germans, was non-existent.

"There was an American doctor with us who had been taken prisoner and was sort of looking after the POWs."

White says one visitor to his work camp surprised and amused him. He was a German Luftwaffe pilot from New York City who spoke impeccable English.

"He heard that there were American POWs near where he was stationed and he came up to our work camp, stood outside the fence and talked to us for about half an hour one day," White relates. "He told us how his family came to the U.S. I'm not sure if he was born here or not, but he spoke perfect English and talked to one of our guys about places around New York. He said in 1939 his family sent him back to Germany to visit his grandparents. By then Hitler would not let anyone return and he was inducted into the Luftwaffe. I remember him saying how he knew they would never send him to the American front because he would take the plane to the American lines and land it. He was certain that he would be going to the Russian front."

With dreams of escape on the minds of many American prisoners of war, White says he never seriously considered it.

"I could see where you had chances to escape," he says. "But where are you going to go? There's no place to go. You don't have any outside contacts and you don't know the language.

"But we did have two guys who made up their minds that they wanted out," White continues. "You get to a point like that— frustrated. They said they were going to try and escape. So we watched the guards. They took roll call twice a day; once in the morning and again in the evening. They would come in through this big door, through a barbed-wire enclosure, which had a lock on it, and on Saturday nights they got into a bad habit of coming in through that big door and not locking it behind them.

"So we saved these guys as much food as we could. One night, as soon as the guards came through this big door, it was dark in that area, these two guys went past them and got behind the door. When the guards went past, the two went out through the door, underneath the barbed wire and got going. When the guards came in for their count, we moved around a lot so they didn't really get a good count. Then they left. The next morning, I remember it was a Sunday, they started counting us. We were trying to move around to keep them from getting the right count again, but then all of a sudden they realized that two men were missing."

Local civilians, after a day or two, saw the escapees in a field and reported them to the Germans.

"They did bring them back, but took them away and I never saw them again after that. I don't know what happened to them."

As Germany's lines in the east collapsed in front of the Russian onslaught, White's days as a POW were numbered.

"We knew the Russians were coming," he says. "We would get bits and pieces of news. They weren't that close that we could hear them, but they were in eastern Prussia and coming our way. So the Germans started to round us up and move us west. Everyday we were on the move, about as far as you could walk in a day's time, for two or three months. At night they would find a farm and pull us into a barn to sleep."

About 300 prisoners were in his group headed westward, walking nearly 600 miles before being liberated by an American armored column near Frankfurt on April 13, 1945, the happiest Friday the 13th in his life.

"We heard firing and saw fighter planes overhead so we knew Americans weren't too far away. These fellows in jeeps and armored cars came up and found us. The German guards turned their weapons over to us. There was one guard who had a dog and it was mean. He'd sic that dog on the prisoners. A lot of the guys were determined to do something to this dog. But before they had a chance to do anything to it, the guard shot the dog himself."

The former prisoners were told by the Americans to stay where they were until other U.S. units arrived.

"We were in a little hamlet with about half a dozen houses. The Americans didn't have any rations to give us so we found some chickens and cooked up a big meal that night. Then we moved into these civilian houses and stayed there for a couple of days."

Inside one of them, White located a pencil and paper and wrote a letter to his parents. It survives, on very thin, onion-skin type paper, and reflects the gladness a freed person would feel after spending more than a year behind barbed wire and enduring an arduous trek by foot to ultimate freedom. This is what was written in its entirety:

☆ ☆ ☆ Sunday Morning 8:30 ☆ ☆ ☆
April 15, 1945

Dear Mom & Dad,

I guess this is the happiest letter I have ever written. Friday, April 13, at 3:00 P.M., we were recaptured by our own boys. I really felt like crying when I saw our own tanks coming down the road toward us. Many of the boys did for that matter and the fellows that recaptured us were just as happy as we were. The rest of my life I know that Friday the 13th will be my lucky day. We are patiently awaiting our return to good old America, a heaven on earth, your lesson, after spending 15 months in this damn Germany.

I guess you have been worrying about me for the last two

months. Well the complete story will have to wait until I get home but here is a brief summary: If you didn't know we were imprisoned near the Polish border about 90 miles from Danzig. The Russians made a big offensive and the Germans moved us about 900 kilometers by foot to western Germany where we were so lucky to be recaptured by our boys. We walked for eight weeks. But every step was worth it just to see good old American doughboys again. Well I've seen most of Germany and I don't believe this war can go on much longer. These "Dutchmen" have practically nothing left. The GI's are on the move now and really traveling.

I don't know how long it will be before we are sent back to the states but two Generals told us yesterday, it would be as soon as possible. So maybe I'll see you before long.

We've had some pretty tough times in our imprisonment in Germany but they are all over now. I have so much to tell you but it will have to wait. Tell everyone I said "hello" and I wish I could write to all. This letter is being written on captured German stationery. I doubt if the censors can read this letter. I'm so excited I'm just scribbling it out. Give my love to all. I must say so long now.

Your loving son,
Jimmy

Soon after writing the letter, the men were moved by trucks to an airfield from where they flew to France, staying there a few more days before being sent home from Camp Lucky Strike in Le Havre, one of the major embarkation points for returning GIs. He boarded a hospital ship on April 27th, which first made port in Southampton, England, to pickup wounded soldiers, and arrived at Staten Island in New York City harbor on May 13th. From there White was sent to Fort Dix in New Jersey, given a sixty-day furlough to visit family and friends at home, and ordered to Atlantic City for seven days of testing.

"We stayed at one of those big hotels on the boardwalk. I had my teeth fixed and my eyes tested. That's when I finally got glasses again."

The hotel that White stayed in was one of the most impressive at the time: the Hotel Dennis. It housed the Army Ground Forces Redistribution Station where men were examined to determine their fitness for future assignments. Following these tests, White was sent to Camp Livingston, Louisiana, to help train recruits in a rifle company.

"While I was at Camp Livingston the war in Japan ended and

they started closing down these camps because they weren't needed," he says. "I still didn't have enough points to get out of the army so I was shipped to Camp Roberts, California, to train those headed over to occupy Japan."

White was discharged in December, 1945. Looking back on his war service, he is amazed that he returned home while so many others didn't.

"I don't consider myself a hero," he says. "The heroes were the ones who didn't make it back. Pauline (his wife) always said that God had a purpose, that I was meant to look after my mom and dad, and then to look after my mother after my dad died. I don't know what it was. But I do feel a little bit guilty. Maybe I should have died there, too, along the Rapido. But that's fate. You don't know what's going to happen in life."

THE 88

The most successful artillery piece of the war began as a German anti-aircraft gun. It could throw a shell along a ruler-straight line further and with more velocity than any weapon with a similar mission in any Allied arsenal. It was intended to reach altitudes that Allied bombers flew at. And it shot down Allied planes in huge numbers.

The 88 was as transportable as much smaller caliber weapons, but it had a much stronger punch. When it reached the battlefronts of Europe and Africa, all it took was a few turns of the elevation control to turn the 88 into a formidable anti-tank gun. This occurred at a time when tanks and anti-tank weapons were frequently no more than 37mm in caliber.

The 88 stopped thousands of British, Russian, and American tanks in their treads throughout the war. Eventually, low-silhouette anti-tank models and tank-turret variations were deployed. By contrast, the very formidable Russian T-34 began the war with a 52mm main gun. It didn't take the Red Army long to switch to a bigger 90mm weapon. The classic Sherman tank was generally under-equipped with a 75mm weapon.

The 88 had a third mission, precision infantry support. It's accuracy and devastating power could pinpoint targets with minimum barrages.

THE ODYSSEY OF
ED (DOGGIE) GRAJEK
by Bill Houlihan

This is the unique story of one U.S. Army soldier in the Asiatic Pacific Theater in World War II who left his assigned non-combat duties, on two separate occasions, to fight alongside his friends in the U.S. Marine's Third Division. Edwin Grajek ("Doggie" as he was affectionately called) accompanied the Marines into battle in the campaigns on Bougainville (1943) and Guam (1944). What motivated him to seek combat and possible death or injury? He enlisted in the U.S. Army in 1942 to fight, not to be assigned to non-combat duties. So here are a few of the highlights of this American's career during World War II.

Ed Grajek was a young eighteen-year-old patriot when he enlisted in the U.S. Army on September 23, 1942. His first choice was the U.S. Marine Corps. However, his boyhood friend was unable to pass the Marine physical, so both of them enlisted in the Army. On April 30, 1942, Ed sailed for the Asiatic Pacific Theater, where he was assigned to a non-combat unit in the coast artillery in the New Hebrides.

Boredom with non-combat duties quickly set in. Then he met up with some Marines from the Third Marine Division, who were in the New Hebrides for training prior to the invasion of Bougainville in the Solomon Islands. Once again Ed was fired up with a desire for combat. So, when the Marines sailed to Bougainville, Ed stowed away and became part of the Marine division. He landed on the island alongside his Marine buddies in October 1943. After being apprised that he had a stow-away Army soldier in his command on November 1, 1943, the commanding officer assigned Ed to one of the Marine platoons in the front lines, where he participated in five major battles with the Japanese. Quickly he was affectionately nicknamed "Doggie" (name for an Army infantryman), which followed him throughout his careers with the Marines. During one of the battles, "Doggie" received a minor wound to the jaw which was not reported. Apparently, he was concerned about being taken off combat status. On December 27, 1943, Doggie was transferred back to the Army and became Private Grajek once again. He was transferred to the field artillery and performed combat duties with them until February, 1944. On that date he began his tour of hospitals in New Caledonia and Guadalcanal, due to infection of his wounded jaw and other minor ailments. Upon discharge from the hospital, Ed was assigned to a replacement battalion on Guadalcanal.

Once again boredom with non-combatant status set in on Private Grajek. That is until he met up with some of his old buddies from the Third Marine Division. They told him that the division was once again preparing for an invasion of some island. So for a second time in his military career, Ed stowed away with the Marine division as they left for the invasion of Guam. He was in the initial landing force and served heroically until D-Day plus three when he received a severe wound to the left shoulder. This ended his combat days and he was evacuated to the U.S. for a long recuperation period.

The above saga is a summary of Edwin (Doggie) Grajek, obviously a great American. The writer of this narrative is a close friend of Ed's and had to wheedle and needle him to tell his remarkable tale before time erased his presence.

To end this story, one must consider the position of the U.S. Army when Ed twice stowed away with the Marines for the sole purpose of fighting in this war. We can surmise, in view of the inter-service rivalry existing at that time, the Army was happy to *loan* this well-trained soldier to the Marines in their frontline assaults on the enemy.

MARINE DASHES THROUGH GUNFIRE

JOHN WAS A SAILOR
by Philip White

When I was a kid, during World War II, my sister met Gunner's Mate John Fitzsimmons, the man she would spend the rest of her life with. At the time, though, it looked like that wouldn't be very long.

John was in the Navy. He was part of a Naval gun crew assigned to a new civilian transport, a Liberty ship. U-boat wolf packs were bleeding each convoy. And the Navy hoped that posting a 3″ gun in a sheet metal tub ... or perhaps two of them would help give a freighter a fighting chance.

What a 3″ shell could do to stop a torpedo was a question no one asked. But if a U-boat commander *did* stay on the surface, and *if* the freighter had a shot, John and his crewmates were there to take it.

Truth was, John's crew and all the others probably had no chance at all of sinking a U-boat. But they hoped to make the U-boat's crew blink by shooting like crazy. They would also throw star shells in the general vicinity of a sighting so the convoy escorts could come in, find the U-boat and really do some harm.

John didn't know it, no one did, but the U-boat crews called this period of the war "The Second Happy Time." The first time was early in the war. Allied equipment left over from the World War I just couldn't stop the U-boats. In 1943, a huge number of Allied escort ships had been reassigned to the North African operations. The U-boats came back to the Atlantic with a vengeance.

John's first and second crossings were easy. The ships he was on were deep in the convoy, and they made it across safely. His luck didn't hold.

On the third convoy, his ship, carrying trucks and general cargo, was near the front, outside edge of the box. The ships sailed head-on into a line of U-boats waiting for them. His ship was hit in the first crisscrossing spread of torpedoes. The ship started to go down fast by the bow.

The crew in the forward gun-tub was gone. John was in the

aft-tub. And they never got off a shot. The merchant crew, who until now had been a whiney bunch of complainers, reacted like a well-trained Navy crew. No panic. No wasted motions. They got one boat lowered and away and a collapsible tossed over the side. Sixteen men had just died. Four of them from the forward gun crew. Everyone else got off the ship before it went under.

They sat in the water as the convoy zigged past them. Three more ships went down that night . . . and one more the next morning. A Destroyer Escort picked them up after thirteen hours in the water. The convoy commander must have thought the wolf pack had been dispersed. A few fast-moving escorts followed the convoy to prevent an attack from the rear. After a few passes, there were no signs, no echoes. So the DE stopped to pickup John and the others. And took two torpedoes from a very patient U-boat.

There were lots more casualties. From both crews.

Three days in a lifeboat later, a British corvette picked them up and within a week he was England. He was then reassigned to another ship leaving Scotland for Murmansk, in Russia.

More U-boats. Rumors of surface ships (but they stayed rumors). And now German aircraft flying out of Norway made life pretty miserable. His ship was hit and was forced to drop behind the convoy. That meant every German plane that couldn't get a shot at the convoy took out his frustration by bombing John's ship.

They ran out of ammunition and saw smoke several times. But he never knew if they shot anything down. Finally, the ship's engine...damaged beyond repair, broke down completely.

The captain was able to beach the ship about sixty miles out of port. Most of the cargo was off-loaded by lighters. When the civilian and naval crews came ashore, the Russians arrested them. After all, they didn't have permission to be in that part of Russia. And some of them were serving in the military of a foreign power.

It took an amazing amount of red-in-the-face screaming confrontations before they were released to the naval attaché in Murmansk. The crews were billeted on a returning ship as quickly as possible. That last ship made it back to Britain, but it was also hit a few times.

John finished the war in the Pacific, and came back to marry my sister. He's long retired now. A grandfather. And he and his family live in Nevada, a desert state. I understand perfectly.

A RAINY NIGHT ON NEW BRITAIN

by Philip White

☆ ☆ ☆

This story was told to me by my father-in-law, PFC Herbert Blinder, who I called Dad. When I met him he was around fifty. A soft-spoken, easy-going guy with a rock-solid work ethic, he had a sense of fairness that was at the core of his being.

Most of the fighting was over. But there were still broken-up Japanese units straggling around the interior. Each night the sounds of rifles and Thompsons got further and further away.

Dad was in a rifle company. When I asked the question that perhaps should not be asked, "Did you kill anyone?" he just said, "Look, we all shot at them. There were bodies all over the place when the shooting stopped. Let's leave it at that."

One night, his unit was standing down at what passed for a large camp. It was a jungle trail that someone once dropped supplies off at the side. After a few months of supplies being dropped off, picked up, moved around, a whole camp evolved. Medic tents, motor pool, radio tent and by now, the supply dumps, had grown barbed wire fences and gates. And at one of these gates, Private Blinder had the bad luck to draw guard duty one miserable night.

About 0130 hours, Dad saw two shapes, in ponchos, walking up the path that led to his post. He challenged them to halt and give the password. They told him to "**** off" and kept on coming. They sounded like American's and that kept them alive. Just as well. They were two officers who he didn't recognize. And from the condition of their uniforms, they were not from a unit that had been in combat. They identified themselves as being from a unit further back down the trail.

They needed to "check" if the right equipment had been delivered. And if there were "mis-shipments" they had to correct them, and bring important materials back.

Courtesy of National Archives

GI'S IN THE SOUTH PACIFIC

Officers? In the middle of the night? No paper. No work detail. No password. No way! There was a small heap of captured Japanese weapons and gear. Mostly stuff that combat troops had acquired and put aside. Dad realized that that's what these officers wanted. Nambu pistols, swords, and bayonets commanded good money back in Pearl and even more in the States.

Dad wouldn't step aside. If it was a combat situation and they needed something to fight with, sure. But these officers were thieves. One of them ordered Dad to step aside. Dad chambered a round. They told him he was under arrest. He told them that they were. One of them reached for his side-arm. Dad put a bullet into that officer's boot.

The shot brought out about fifty men, all with weapons. The "officer" with the shot boot was lucky, the bullet just left a burn mark between his toes.

By that time, Dad's lieutenant had arrived. The officers wanted Dad arrested and they still wanted to get into the dump. One of them was actually looking at the pile of Japanese gear. Dad's lieutenant said "sure, he'd arrest him." But since they were breaking into a supply column and offered resistance to the guard on duty, they would be arrested too.

"Can I shoot the other one?" Dad asked. "They could both put in for Purple Hearts."

The officer looked at the two scavengers and said, "Wait twenty seconds. Then anyone you see on the trail isn't one of us."

Dad started counting. By fifteen, the trail was empty.

In the 1980s, when he was already a grandfather, he told me this story.

"Would you really have shot them?" I asked.

"I would have put the Holland Tunnel in their chests," he said. I saw something of the young man my father-in-law once was. He was a soldier.

MIRACLE OF CONSTRUCTION

by George A. Larson

George W. Larson, after completing his United States Navy
basic and advanced training posing for a photograph
at his home in Altoona, Iowa.

M y father, George W. Larson, was assigned to the 135th
United States Naval Construction Battalion, better known as
the "Seabees." The Seabees became famous during World War II,
building military facilities around the world, earning a name for
their ability to complete a job, referred to as "Can Do!"

The 135th arrived at the southern end of Tinian Island on the
morning of October 24, 1944. George was in the second group of
Seabees to go over the ship's side. They climbed down cargo nets

into bobbing Higgins Landing Boats, waiting below, which took them to the beach. He was completely equipped as a combat soldier, loaded down with a full combat pack, carrying a loaded carbine. He looked like a U.S. Marine, not a construction worker.

As soon as the Seabees hit the island, they began unloading their heavy equipment, to begin turning the island into a large airfield complex. It was a week before George got a few hours' break, hitching a ride in a jeep for the short but rough trip into the island's main town—referred to as "Tinian Town,"—which had been almost totally destroyed by the U.S. Navy's prebombardment. George witnessed first-hand the destructiveness of the battleship's sixteen-inch guns, which left only roofless buildings, piles of rubble, partially cleared streets, and the naked steel frameworks of the destroyed sugar mill complex. He was on the island to turn destruction into a major U.S. Army Air Force, U.S. Navy, and port supply facility. The airfields were to be prepared for the four-engine Boeing B-29 Superfortresses, the long-range bombers that later would be used to bomb the Japanese Home Islands.

"The Miracle of Construction" on Tinian was an immense project, building six 8,500-foot runways, especially thick to accommodate the combat loaded B-29s. To support B-29 operations, Seabees built twenty-nine miles of connecting taxiways, bomber hardstands, two fighter runways, over 1,000 buildings of every type, fuel and ammunition storage areas, along with everything needed to support an air war against Japan. The effort of 12,000 Seabees, 13,000 Navy, and 21,500 Army troops and engineers combined to move over 11,000,000 cubic yards of earth and coral on the island. Tinian was soon known as "the biggest airport in the world." Toward the end of World War II, the pace of B-29 operations became staggering as the number and strength of Superfortress raids intensified.

North Field consisted of four parallel runways, and was to base the USAAF's B-29s. West Field, with an additional two runways, would base the U.S. Navy's B-24 patrol aircraft. North Field was exceptionally large, designed to hold hundreds of B-29s and their crews, which would attack strategic targets in Japan, hopefully forcing Japan to surrender without an invasion.

George worked on North Field, in many different capacities, as directed by the battalion commander. After assisting in unloading the unit's heavy construction equipment and supplies, he was assigned to direct the constant stream of dump trucks moving from the huge coral pits around the island to North Field, which carried tons of fill material needed to level the runways and taxiways. He had to wear goggles to keep dust out of the eyes and a wet cloth over his mouth to keep from choking. It was hard and dirty work, dangerous among the moving trucks and low visibility. He constantly dodged trucks to keep from being run over.

Construction went on twenty-four hours a day, in rain or in clear weather. At night, portable electric generators were positioned along the runway construction areas, which could be switched off at the first sound of approaching Japanese Betty twin-engine bombers. When the bombers approached Tinian, Seabees dove into prepared slit trenches, keeping their heads down until the air raid was over. Once, George dove into a trench as a bomber roared down the runway he was working on, strafing men and equipment. George heard the sound of bullets smacking into the grader vacated a few seconds before.

The biggest irritant was not Japanese air attacks, but heavy tropical rains which turned the construction and camp sites into a sea of sticking and sucking mud. Seabees were issued rain ponchos, but hardly ever used them because of the island's hot and humid climate. Once the 135th completed their Quonset hut camp, the rain and mud was somewhat easier to handle and live with. Also, once the main roads were hard surfaced, it became a smooth operation to move heavy construction equipment from one part of the island to the other, speeding construction, allowing them to meet tight construction time tables.

George also worked on one of the runway finishing crews, after his assignment directing dump trucks. He drove a slow-moving road grader, down one of the long 8,500 foot runways, scrapping the coral smooth, almost to grade level. It was not unusual for large pieces of unbroken coral (the Seabees used a crusher to pulverize the coral before it was hauled to the runways for spreading) to appear in the runway surface. Grader operators would stop and almost instantly a special work crew, spaced out along the runway, would approach with picks and shovels, and dig out the chunk of coral, rolling it off the runway. The hole was filled with crushed coral, tamped, allowing grading to resume. At the same time, salt water was sprayed on the coral, rolled, followed by spiked rollers, and then graded again. The process was repeated over and over until the runways were smooth, to grade level, and had hard packed surfaces.

George watched many B-29s returning home to North Field from bombing strikes against Japan, before Iwo Jima was invaded, secured, and a B-29 airstrip completed. It was heartbreaking for George to watch the aircraft struggle to reach the safety of North Field. One night, George watched as the ground crew personnel turned on powerful searchlights along the runway edges and pointed them straight up, giving the B-29 pilots a visual approach to North Field, which increased their chances of landing safely. Some of the returning B-29s were on fire, either from battle damage or from overheated engines which froze and caught fire, and could not be extinguished by the crew. These B-29s often missed the runway on the first pass, so they would attempt to climb up, bank around over the Saipan Channel to the north, and set up for a short circuit to return to the runway. George and other Seabees would stop working and talk out loud, urging the badly damaged B-29s to stay in the air, as the crew frantically attempted to reach the safety of the runway. Most B-29s made it, but for those that did not, it was usually because the pilots misjudged their landing approach, or as a result of engine failure or control surface damage, they were unable to properly line up for a landing. These B-29s usually crashed into the runway, ripping off their landing gear, sliding along the runway until stopping, exploding in bright orange flames. Some made it out of the aircraft and others did not. It was sad to see the deaths of so many brave airmen. Because of the Superfortress's tendency to burst into flames after crash landing or on abort-takeoff crashes, crews nicknamed the aircraft "Flying Coffins." The strain on men watching these landings was sobering. This was an unforgettable view of the air war against Japan, up close and in person, something George only reluctantly talked about long after World War II.

SEABEES

Construction Battalions were one of the most successful American innovations of the war in the Pacific. They could build runways, clear harbors, and construct entire military bases while battles raged around them.

During the Guadalcanal Campaign, Seabees pounded out several airfields complete with protective revetments, fuel, repair, and ammo depots, all within range of enemy forces. In contrast and in relative safety, Japanese engineers were able to expand only one runway during the same period.

Seabees would descend on a building site with much the same fervor as the marines who had hit the beaches only hours before. Their working locations were usually in or close to combat zones. Their timetables were always short and conditions were always tough. Yet they never failed to answer, "The difficult we do immediately, the impossible takes a little longer."

THE DAMN CRABS

by Fran More

M y father, now in his late eighties, was stationed at a remote airfield in New Caledonia as a plane mechanic in the 1940s. He didn't speak of those days much, but one winter afternoon he became agitated over on the couch as we all watched a science show on TV about land crabs: a terrible look of vexation and hatred filled his face as he shakily pointed at the screen.

"I killed so damn many of those things in the war it's a crime," he announced with unusual venom in his usually calm voice. The TV show was shocking: thousands of land crabs covering beaches and highways, forests of palm trees, bridges, even an airfield somewhere.

"Gosh, did they bite you?" I asked, horrified.

"If those damn things ever got a hold of you they never let go. Hurts like hell. You have to beat 'em to a pulp before they let go, and it isn't easy. They got into everything. Every morning when we went out to service the planes, the engines would be full of 'em. If we tried to jerk them out they'd injure all the connectors and wiring, then we'd have extra repairs to do. We couldn't burn 'em out with blowtorches or we'd risk an explosion or maybe damaging small parts. Yet, every morning we spent half the day removing all sizes of crabs from the plane engines before we could do our work. You couldn't reach up anywhere you couldn't see without worrying about getting bit or pinched. There was no way to keep them off the field, and they'd think the tires were trees and just climb on up into whatever protected spot they could find. We couldn't close up the openings they got in by. We couldn't stay up all night guarding the field beating them with crowbars in the dark. Some of the planes had to sit there quite a while waiting to be serviced and the damn crabs would just climb over any makeshift barrier we thought would help. We were always worried we'd missed one and it would some-how cause an engine failure, which would then be our fault."

He rolled over in disgust, muttering. I changed the channel.

Courtesy of National Archives

INFANTRY COMING ASHORE AT BUTARITARI

GLOOMY SUNDAY

Written by
GILBERT J. HELWIG TO HIS FATHER
Submitted by Edward J. Helwig

☆ ☆ ☆

SEPTEMBER 11, 1945

Dear Dad,

This is, I believe, the first uncensored letter I have written to you since June of 1943—and, yet, either I have become so used to censorship that I have grown to ignore it, or else its limitations were not important, for I can't think of a single thing to say which I could not have told you before. No, that is not true. There is one thing. I have never told you about: "Gloomy Sunday." I think it likely that you never heard about it back in the States.

"Gloomy Sunday," as we came to call it, occurred on the Sunday following Easter last year—about April 16, 1944—at Saidor. It had started to rain Saturday night and Sunday dawned overcast and gloomy. All morning it drizzled intermittently, but the P-47s and A-20s stationed at Saidor had taken off on their regular strikes. By noon the ceiling was zero and the rain was falling in a steady, monotonous beat. As I left the mess hall, I heard a dull steady drone overhead. "Sounds like heavies," I said to someone. "Yeah," was the reply. "B-24s probably."

As I walked back toward the tent I noticed that the drone continued and intensified—that there were quite a large number of aircraft in the dull black overcast of clouds—and they were circling the traffic pattern. Something was wrong down at the strip. The planes weren't able to come in for a landing.

Normally on Sundays only a small crew went to the line, but just about this time, one of the fellows in the outfit came through the area on the run. "All men on crash crews report to the motor pool at once!" he shouted. Pausing only to throw my mess kit in the tent, I ran to the motor pool where the fellows were loading on to trucks.

As we rode toward the strip the sound of motors overhead became heavier and more varied, and we knew that in the sky above us (although not a single plane could be seen) were a large number of bombers and fighters circling the landing strip in a macabre pattern, trying to land.

At the strip, as we readied ambulances, crash wagons, and tractors, we began to piece together the story. Practically every operational aircraft in the Fifth Air Force had been committed that morning to a large scale, long-range strike at Hollandia in support of ground operations in that sector. The weather, bad all day, had gotten steadily worse and it became practically impossible for the planes to return to their bases at Nadzab on the other side of the Finnisusterre mountain range. They had headed instead for Saidor—the nearest and most advanced American base. Saidor was itself closed in, and not equipped to handle the additional traffic. There was but a single strip at Saidor, and not even a level field which could be used as a crash strip.

When we got to the strip, the tower controllers were trying to bring in the ships as quickly as they could, priority in landing being given to the heavy bombers. Meanwhile the others continued to circle about. We knew they were getting low on gas. Occasionally a 24 would come limping in, loom low past the tower and an eerie purple-red flare would slowly drop. Wounded aboard! It would take priority in the landing pattern.

The planes, meanwhile, continued to land and taxi toward the parking area. Because of the miserable weather (and the crippled condition of many of the planes) each landing was hazardous. Every time one of the big bulkish 24s loomed out of the murk at the end of the runway, not a person seemed to breathe until its wheels had successfully touched the steel matting and it had begun to roll to a safe landing. Then everyone would release his breath in a sort of grunt. As the planes would roll past the tower you could see the sickly grins on the faces of the crew. One waist gunner, I remember, went by shaking his hands over his head like a boxer in a gesture of relief and sheer excitement.

The sky kept growing darker and it was raining harder. Under the dismal sky the monotonous drone overhead seemed foreboding; it seemed to speak of impending disaster. So far all the planes had landed safely.

Then it happened! A B-25 was coming in at one end of the runway when a P-38 ran out of gas and tried to come in on a dead stick landing at the other end of the runway. No doubt the pilot of the 38 thought he could swerve from the strip after he had cut down his speed. Perhaps he could not even see the 25. At any rate, they met head-on in the middle of the strip and burst into flames.

The crash truck screamed out onto the field while the tower flashed a red light to the other ships in the traffic pattern. As some men went in with fire extinguishers others in asbestos suits went into the flames to try to pull out the crew; others tried to fasten chains to the landing gear to pull the planes from the strip. As the big wrecker began to tow the 25 off, the landing gear pulled out from the nose of the ship and the blackened rolled-up bit of crisp which had been the bombardier fell to the ground. The planes were virtually consumed before the flames could be extinguished. A bulldozer was brought onto the strip and the wreckage—bodies and all—were just scraped off the strip. It was important to clear the strip fast. We walked in a line across the strip picking up fragments of metal which the bulldozer had left. The fellow walking next to me picked up a blackened shoe—with a foot in it.

The next plane which came in was a 24. It landed safely, but then struck a piece of sharp metal on the strip which someone had overlooked, blew a tire and careened from the runway striking our wrecker. Then began a series of crashes. An A-20 came in on its belly. The landing gear of a P-47 folded as it hit the strip. There were near accidents—and one I remember as the most beautiful, most foolhardy bit of flying I have ever witnessed. A B-25 was coming in for a landing. It had nearly touched its wheels to the end of the runway, when a P-38 above ran out of gas. The P-38 pilot put his plane into a dive toward the strip and without putting his wheels down, pulled the ship out of the dive just in time to clear the B-25, hop in front of it onto the runway, landing on his belly and kicking his ship into a skid which brought him off the runway just in time get out of the way of the B-25. The P-38 pilot crawled out of his cockpit unhurt and grinning.

Because of the crashes which tied up the runway, orders were given to one entire squadron of P-38s to go out over the bay and jettison their ships.

It was late at night when the last ship had been "sweated in."

Everywhere one looked there were crippled and crashed planes along the side of the strip. Many had flak and bullet holes in them. Some were mere heaps of rubble, little bonfires burning. Out in the bay there had crashed, deliberately crashed, thirteen sleek and beautiful P-38s and four A-20s.

We were cold and chilled and tired and wet and covered with mud from head to foot. But mostly we were sick with horror at the destruction we had helplessly witnessed. We went back to the line where the cooks had set up boilers of coffee. I couldn't get the smell of burnt flesh out of my nose.

Saidor was a beautiful base. It was ideal for living; it was in many respects the finest air base in New Guinea. In all the time that it was operational it was closed only ten hours because of bad weather. Those ten hours all came on one Sunday in April, 1944. They cost nearly half of the operational strength of the entire Fifth Air Force. The headlines you were reading back home then told of the ease and dispatch with which the landings at Hollandia and Aitape were proceeding. There were some other things I had thought of to write but I guess I had better save them for another letter.

No further news on our going home status, although the rumors continue apace. Don't expect me so quickly as the daily announcements from the W.D. might lead you to think.

Affectionately,
Gil

BEN PRESTON,
FEARLESS BEN—1944

by Richard Duckett

By the time I met him he had already won the Navy's highest decoration twice, the Navy Cross. He also had a chestful of other decorations; the Silver Star; the Distinguished Flying Cross; the Air Medal. In his dress whites, there was precious little room for his wings of gold, the badge of the naval aviator.

He took offence at all who called him a navy pilot. The proper term for all who wore the wings was "naval aviator."

He was commissioned before the war and after flight school at Pensacola, Florida. He was assigned as a scout pilot attached to the cruiser *Augusta*, flying float-equipped Curtiss SOC-2S, from a catapult over the number three eight-inch gun turret. His best memory of that duty occurred during the cruise taking President Roosevelt to Argentia, Newfoundland, for his historic meeting with Prime Minister Winston Churchill, before the U.S. was involved in World War II.

The ship's captain was a latecomer to naval aviation, one J. J. Clark, a full-blooded American Indian who thirty years before had made his way through the United States Naval Academy at Annapolis. Jocko, as he preferred to be known ("the Indian" behind his back) had a ferocious temper and didn't suffer fools.

In order to continue to receive his flight pay, a considerable sum for a captain, Clark had to put in his minimum four hours a month. So on a quiet but bleak afternoon when he was sure the politicos were at work, Jock ordered his Exec to put a plane in the water and dragoon a check pilot.

When the ship's speakers boomed out a summons for Ensign Benjamin Preston to the starboard catapult in flight gear, Ben shot out of his bunk in the junior officer's quarters like a scalded cat. Flight operations certainly weren't on the schedule. Ben's mind tossed about the chances of a declared war.

Nevertheless he appeared as ordered and was shocked to find his captain in the front seat. This was not the correct drill. Ben's boss, head of the department, was a full lieutenant with vast experience and had always been the captain's check pilot. In truth Jock Clark was never to fly alone. Nobody trusted him, least of all himself.

At any rate Ben settled himself into the rear seat where he could watch the captain's every move. Clark went through the proper drill and got the engine started. The Exec brought the ship into the proper angle into the wind. Ben carefully got his hands and feet just a smidgen away from the controls. Clark shoved the throttle home and as soon as the roar satisfied him brought his hand down in a chop and the catapult officer shot them into the air.

A hundred yards on the SOC settled on the water, engine blasting away. Clark turned to Ensign Preston and shouted something Ben couldn't make out. Clark turned back to his objective of getting the SOC airborne. At full throttle Capt. J. J. Clark went thundering around Argentia Bay until finally a timid Preston, terrified of the consequences, reached around the captain's body and advanced the spark control, hoping that the captain wouldn't notice. The airplane, now under full power duly took notice and soared into the air.

Captains don't usually speak to ensigns particularly about captains' faults so Ben never found out whether the captain noticed.

The war commenced that December for the U.S. and Ben spent time as an instructor and with a dive bombing squadron in another group before joining VB-18 before it began its fateful cruise on the U.S.S. *Intrepid*. By then he was a full two striper. On joining, the Skipper, a full commander, assigned him duty as operations officer, third in command and nominated him a strike leader. VB-18 started with six six-plane divisions and any two constituted a strike group.

I would like to say that I followed him on many a strike in the Pacific that Summer and Fall and that I didn't enjoy any of them.

Ben went on to win two more Navy Crosses and he even led me to one. I enjoy his friendship. We meet at the reunions with dwindling numbers and he still frightens me.

SAILOR
by Michael D. Ekern

After forty hours with the clatter of four eighteen-foot diesel engines making written notes necessary for communication, in weather so overcast, "you could have made fogballs," Carl Storm got word that the U.S.S. *Thomas* was going to ram a German U-boat.

He thought it was a joke.

"I fell backward against one of the railings," Storm says. "The next thing I knew, all the deck plates were sliding forward. I was worried about getting my feet cut off."

The *Thomas* had slammed into the German submarine, riding on to her for forty feet. Topside, the situation was macabre.

"Our guns put their guns out of commission and by the time we were going in to ram, they were abandoning ship," Storm says. Richie, the barber, was manning one of the 20 mm. guns. "The [captain] hollered cease fire . . . but not Richie," Storm intones, shaking his head. "He was plucking them off." One German, minus his head, jumped in the water and swam away. The sub sank in minutes.

Today, all that remains of U-233 is a scrap of steel in Annapolis, Maryland, and an enlarged frame of 8 mm. film showing the bow of the *Thomas* about to crush her hull. That picture, as well as shots of the *Thomas*, hangs on Storm's apartment wall. If you ask him about those pictures, he'll straighten just a little and tell you about a time fifty-seven years past.

Carl Storm was a sailor, assigned to the U.S.S. *Thomas*, a destroyer escort designed to hunt German U-boats. The *Thomas*, 308 feet long and capable of twenty knots (twenty-three miles per hour), was driven by four sixteen-cylinder diesel engines capable of 6,000 horsepower. Storm's job was to maintain those engines buried deep inside the hull. Generating that much power could raise the engine room temperature to 120 degrees Fahrenheit. It was also loud.

"[You] couldn't hear yourself think," Storm marvels. "Even with the cotton in your ears, it was an hour after you got out of there before you could hear right. I was down there sixteen, eighteen, twenty hours a day. When we [went] to battle stations I always went down there. Then you had to stand regular watches."

Miserable conditions do not excuse a sailor from his work.

Seamen spent four hours on watch, performing equipment checks and training for combat, and eight hours off, eating such treats as fresh rolls and hamburger, sleeping and studying technical manuals. The worst shift on the *Thomas*, the exception to the four-hour rule, was 11:30 p.m. to 5:30 a.m. Before going on that watch, sailors ate "lunch." For Storm, those lunches are some of his most pleasant memories.

"They had one guy from Oklahoma that was good on the guitar. And we had an Italian from New York who was on the violin. We had a rebel kid . . . he could play the spoons. We'd play all the local songs. Guys used to get up and come when we went on the midnight watch . . . because we had so much fun."

But life on board the *Thomas* was mostly monotony.

"Untold drills," Storm says, a hint of agitation in his voice. "It was constant drills. Middle of the night, you'd little more get to sleep . . . and the bell would go off. You were to be on your station within minutes."

Combat brought a sharp contrast to the unchanging routine of daily ship life. Ships such as the *Thomas* hunted U-boats with depth charges and devices called hedgehogs. Both are canisters filled with explosive that detonate underwater.

"I knew when them depth charges [were fired] and I knew exactly how long it was going to take them to explode. They'd shake the whole ship."

The concussion was powerful enough to dislodge three-inch bolts holding the engines down. Storm would prop himself up on railings to take the jolt in his arms, instead of his legs. Then he would go around with a hammer and pound the bolts back into place.

Despite that, Storm says he doesn't regard the combat as the worst part.

"The first cruise you make, you're pretty worried. Nobody wants to die. It finally became a job. You're out in the middle of nowhere and you ain't going to run off and hide. You're there and what is your destiny? If you're going to die, you're going to die."

Death is part of the job for a sailor.

However, his eyes narrow at the thought of the weather. He recalls a squall with winds of 128 knots (147 m.p.h.).

"Three days we were in that sucker. The mast was forty-six or forty-eight feet [high] and [the waves] were breaking way the hell over that. I'll never forget the way that son-of-a-gun rolled. Forty-five degree rolls—that was nothing." He pauses for a moment and a smile breaks across his face. "Never missed a meal."

The end of the war came for Storm, after the ramming of U-233, when he was transferred off the *Thomas*. He was elated at the idea of survival.

"But as I walked off that dock I cried," he says, his lower lip trembling. His voice cracks. "She's home."

Carl Storm missed his ship the way only a sailor could.

KAMIKAZES

The word itself means "divine wind." It was first used centuries ago when a Mongol invasion fleet was bearing down on Japan. The size of the fleet and numbers of Mongols on board were too much for the Japanese to defend against. But fortune favored the Japanese when a storm swept through the Inland Sea and scattered the invaders.

In 1945, a similar situation was brewing. After the Philippine Campaign, the Imperial Japanese Navy no longer existed beyond a few scattered ships. Their airforce was outmatched in every category. And the army was either bogged down in China, isolated on bypassed islands or in retreat wherever they met advancing Anglo-American troops.

The Japanese reached into the past for a miracle. This time the Divine Wind would be pilots on a mission to sink American ships besieging Okinawa. But planes weren't the only Kamikazes. Motorboats laden with explosives, midget submarines and even the largest battleship in the world, the mighty *Yamato*, would take part.

The Japanese had used some suicide planes earlier in the war and knew they could sink ships. Wave after wave of suicide planes took many Allied ships out of the line. They damaged many and sank a few, while causing thousands of casualties.

At the height of the air assault on the U.S. Navy, the *Yamato* with its huge 18" guns roared into the battle. Its mission was to blast through the U.S. ships, doing as much damage as possible and then, since there was not enough fuel to return to Japan, it was supposed to ram into the beach. Its big guns would become a monstrous artillery platform while the bulk of the crew would wade ashore and re-enforce the garrison. It was never to be.

A U.S. submarine observed the *Yamato* as soon as it left its anchorage. The *Yamato* was hit and sunk by naval aircraft in just twenty minutes.

NEAR MISS
by Michael Staton

The U.S.S. *Evans*, a Fletcher Class destroyer, was forty miles northwest of Okinawa on May 11, 1945. She was steaming in company with the U.S.S. *Hadley* to protect the fleet anchorage from kamikaze raids sent down from mainland Japan. In one of the gun tubs on this tin can was a young man from Middletown, Ohio. Seaman First Class James Staton had joined the Navy in January, 1944, even though he was only seventeen at the time. Now he was responsible for loading 40 mm. ammunition to mount forty-three, one of the five antiaircraft twin machine guns mounted on the ship.

Nearly 150 enemy planes were sent out that morning to destroy ships of the U.S. fleet. Navy and Marine fighter planes were vectored out to intercept and they splashed nearly fifty before the enemy planes found the two destroyers. As all hell broke loose, the distance between *Hadley* and *Evans* grew ever greater. They began to fight for their own lives. The *Evans* shot down eighteen planes (with some assists from *Hadley* and Marine fighter planes), and fought for nearly an hour before being hit port side amidships, which put a hole in the hull at the waterline. Then came another hit on the same side near the engineering room. This caused much more damage. Power was lost to the guns and they had to be fired manually.

The entire complement of the *Hadley*'s guns soon began firing on two diving Jap fighters, one from low on the starboard bow and one from high on the port quarter. Though the barrage was tremendous, both guns hit their targets at nearly the same instant. The first plane crashed into the galley behind the forward stack. He dropped a bomb just before impact and it detonated in the forward fireroom. The second skidded down the starboard side, taking out the boat davit and spreading burning gasoline everywhere.

James Staton was right in the middle of this chaos yet somehow he came through the final two collisions without a scratch. He was one of the lucky ones. Seaman First Class William Urton was thrown over the side while at the 40 mm. gun director port side amidships. He was lost at sea. Three men passing ammunition to mount forty-three were killed, and another was severely burned after two Oscars crashed close to them. Gunner's Mate Third Class Paul Merics, gun captain, and S1c. Staton kept their gun trained along with the injured Voight even though fires had broken out around the mount. These three were the only surviving men from mount forty-three.

U.S. HORNET, 1945

Courtesy of National Archives

A few miles away, Second Lieutenant Raymond N. Wagner and his wingman Second Lieutenant Wendell M. Larson, two Marine pilots, spotted a "Nate" (Ki-27) preparing to make a run on the smoking and almost lifeless *Evans*. Wagner made the first pass but broke off when he couldn't get a good shot in. Larson then got behind the Nate and squeezed off a few rounds from his six .50 caliber machine guns as he tried to line up a good shot. The Nate never wavered and pressed on his attack straight at the bridge of the crippled ship. By this time the fighters were only 2500 yards away from the *Evans*. Gunner's Mate Second Class Michael Keda, gun captain on mount forty-two, alertly took over for his injured trainer and joined the pointer, Seaman First Class Robert Stonelake, in firing their gun in manual at the closing kamikaze. LCS82, a landing craft that had just tied up to the starboard side of the *Evans*, also opened up on the attacker. Hits from Larson's Corsair, the *Evans*, and LCS82 caused the Nate to pitch away from the destroyer at the last moment. The plane passed down the port side just feet away and slammed into the water 250 yards astern of the *Evans*. Larson then winged over and pulled up, narrowly missing the ship's rigging.

I had always been interested in finding out more about my father's wartime experiences. He seldom spoke of them, only when he thought of a funny anecdote. After his death in 1992, I began searching for information on his ship and found the *Evans* Reunion Committee. I attended a reunion in May, 1997, and immediately began to write a historical account of his ship. Along the way I met and spoke with many crew members and their families. One of the most exciting things for me was introducing Mr. Wendell Larson to the surviving crew of the *Evans*. One of the old sailors shook his hand and said, "I've been waiting fifty-four years to say thank you!"

TIMING IS EVERYTHING
by William C. Kempner

I have always been a great adherent to the old maxim that "timing is everything."

In October, 1943, my father, Electrician's Mate Third Class David George Kempner, had enlisted in the Navy and was in boot camp and service school for electrician's mate strikers (now known as EM "A" School) in Newport, Rhode Island. After several postings and redlines, he was stationed at the submarine base at Rodman in the Panama Canal Zone. In late October of 1944, he was on a job repairing a sub when the U.S.S. *Mannert L. Abele* proceeded through the canal. Apparently, they had left Norfolk a bit short-handed and were asking for electrician's mates, and other ratings that they were short of, to come aboard.

At that point, my father had been in the Canal Zone slightly longer than some of the other electrician's mates in his shop, and as a rule, any requests for additional manning took the guys who had been there longest. But, when he could not be found, a friend of his from Newport, a guy from Tennessee with the first name of Lindsey, was sent aboard. When my father returned to his shop, well after the evening meal hours and covered with grease and oily water from having worked in the bilges of the diesel-electric submarine to access its many batteries, he was greeted by his CPO with the question, "where were you?" Being tired, hungry, and filthy (and nineteen years old), my father dropped his tool bag on a work bench and shot the chief a look, and said, "ballroom dancing. Where do you think I was?" The chief let it pass and told him what had transpired, with his friend being sent aboard the *Abele*. My father shrugged, and called it a night.

The U.S.S. *Mannert L. Abele* was to have a rendezvous with destiny. It departed San Diego on January 27, 1945, for the invasion of Iwo Jima, where the ship was involved in heavy shore bombardment and close-support missions. Upon the successful conquest of Iwo

Jima, the *Abele* was detailed to Task Force Fifty-four for the invasion of Okinawa to serve in her pre-determined role as a radar picket ship. On the afternoon of April 12, 1945, while serving in that role about seventy miles northwest of Okinawa, the *Abele* was attacked by three kamikazes at the same time. Two were driven off and one was destroyed. At 2:00 P.M. the ship was attacked by fifteen to twenty-five additional planes and according to report, "was completely surrounded." Yet, the planes remained out of gun range. At 2:40 P.M., three planes broke off and attacked. One was driven off, one was shot down, but the third crashed on the starboard side and penetrated the after engine room where it exploded. The ship immediately lost headway, as the attack had broken the ship's keel, effectively breaking the ship's back. At 2:46 P.M., the U.S.S. *Mannert L. Abele* took a second and fatal hit from a baka bomb—a piloted, rocket-powered glider bomb—that struck the starboard side again, at the waterline, abreast the forward fire room, breaking the ship in two. It lost all power, lights, and communications, and sank almost immediately. As the crew abandoned ship, enemy planes bombed and strafed the survivors in the water. However, two supporting vessels drove off the rest of the planes and managed to rescue a number of survivors. Sadly, Lindsey was not one of them.

My father learned of his friend's passing not long after, and recalled his close call often over the rest of his life. Even facing serious illness toward the end of his life, at age sixty-one in 1987, he would smile slightly, and say "It could have been over a long time ago. I can still remember Lindsey's face, even now. I think of him often. It just wasn't my time."

Like (and perhaps because of) both those men, I served in the U.S. Navy also, making a career of it. I retired in 1994 as a Lieutenant, having served as a Special Operations (diving) Officer, a second-generation navy diver, and a Desert Storm veteran. At this writing (Fall 2000), I have been recalled to service by the governor of New York, to serve as the Flag Secretary for the Commander of the New York Naval Militia, a Rear Admiral. I hope both men would be proud of me. I thank Lindsey, for giving up his future for all of us, and my father, for the many sacrifices he made throughout his life for our family and community. I hope I have proven myself worthy of their sacrifices.

SURVIVOR OF THE MIGHTY *TANG*

by Jesse B. DaSilva

I joined the submarine *Tang* after her second war patrol. I made the third, fourth, and final patrols.

We were on our fifth patrol in the narrow strip of water between the island of Formosa and the China coast on the night of October 24, 1944. We had had a very successful patrol, sinking several ships. We were down to our last two torpedoes and fired these at a crippled transport. The first went straight but the second made a circular run.

I was a Motor Machinist Mate and had left the engine room a few minutes earlier to get a cup of coffee in the crew's mess. Two other men were with me. One had headphones. He was keeping us posted. After the last torpedo was fired we waited for the word "All Ahead Emergency!" and then we got it. The torpedo hit between the after torpedo room and the maneuvering room. Someone dogged down the watertight door between the after and forward engine rooms. The *Tang* was settling quickly by the stern. I clutched a ladder to keep from being pitched off my feet. Water was pouring in from the open doorway that connected the crew's mess with the control room. I thought to myself, "Let's get this door shut." Two or three of us seized the door and with a great effort shoved it closed, cutting off the flow of water.

The Japanese came over us and dropped depth charges for some time. By now we had cleared the partly flooded forward engine room and closed it off. There were now about twenty of us in the mess room and crew's quarters. We knew that we couldn't stay there because of chlorine gas. We knew, too, that our one chance of escape was in reaching the forward torpedo room. But we had to pass through the control room to get there. This meant opening the control room door and for all we knew, it might be flooded. Yet, we had to risk it.

Someone cracked the door…water gushed in…water rose around

our legs then gradually subsided. We discovered that the control room was only partially flooded. One by one, we moved forward, knee deep in water. We filed into the control room and destroyed all secret devices. I noticed at this time the depth gauge was at 180 feet. I thought to myself that there was still a chance if we could reach the escape hatch located in the forward torpedo room. We passed through the officers' quarters and into the torpedo room.

There were already twenty-odd men in the compartment. Our arrival brought the number to forty-five. There were some injured men and the air was foul and breathing was difficult. Everyone was given a Momsen Lung. There had already been several attempted escapes and now they were going to make another. I found myself at the foot of the ladder leading up into the escape trunk.

I heard someone say, "Let's have another man!" I quickly climbed up into the trunk. I was the third man. We still needed one more. Then another stepped to the ladder, climbed in and then we closed the hatch. Everything went just as we were taught at the escape tank back at Pearl Harbor. We flooded the trunk, filled our Momsen Lungs with oxygen, and tested them to see if they were working. As the water rose in the trunk, pressure built up, and breathing became difficult. When the water level reached above the outer door we opened it. Someone had already let out the buoy with a line attached from the previous escapes, and now it was my turn to follow the line to the surface.

I was the third one out. I wrapped my feet around the rope and slowly let myself up, ten feet at a time, stopping and counting to ten each time. About a third of the way up, breathing became more difficult but soon the problem went away and the water became lighter. Suddenly I was on the surface. Nearby and holding onto the buoy were four men who had escaped before me.

We could see the ships we had sunk from the night before. A short time later two more men came up. One was Paul L. Larson, our Chief Pharmacist Mate. He came up right by us but he had difficulty breathing, so we held on to him. The other was one of our Steward Mates. He came up some distance from us and acted like he couldn't swim. As I reached him he disappeared, so I turned to swim back to the others. I didn't realize I had drifted so far. It took a great effort to reach them. I realized that the current was moving out to sea and there would be no chance to make the mainland of

China that we could see off in the distance.

After spending several hours in the water, a Japanese destroyer escort that had been circling the area slowly came over to where we were. It circled us several times and then stopped a short distance away. It then turned its guns toward us. I thought to myself, "Well, this is it . . . they are going to shoot us." But instead, they lowered a small boat, came over, and picked us up.

They took us to their ship, tied our hands behind us, and made us sit on the metal deck in the hot sun. I was surprised to see four other members of our crew on board. This made a total of nine that survived.

One by one, the Japanese took us aside and interrogated us. When it was my turn, they led me to another part of the ship and had me sit down between three of them. They offered me a bowl of rice, but I could not eat it. One of them had an electrical device and he would jab me in the ribs with this and I would twitch and jump. They all thought this was very funny. The one that could speak English carried a large club about the size of a baseball bat. He would ask questions and if he didn't like the answers he would hit me on the head with this bat. After some time, when they figured that I wasn't going to tell them anything, they took me back to the others.

☆ ☆ ☆ Ofuna ☆ ☆ ☆

After a short stay on the nearby island of Formosa, we were separated and put on two different ships. The officers were put on one and the enlisted men on another. There were five of us enlisted men and we were together in the forward hold of a destroyer. It was quite a voyage to Japan. A few of us got sick as the trip was very rough.

When we finally reached Japan we were put on a train in a boxcar and traveled this way for a long time until we reached our destination, the interrogation camp of Ofuna. We were taken from the train and we had to walk in the rain for some distance to the camp. When I had made my escape from the *Tang*, the only piece of clothing I had on was a pair of pants, so all the time we were walking I was very wet and cold. When we reached the camp my feet were very sore and numb.

They took us into a room where they gave each of us a dry shirt, pants, and a pair of tennis shoes that were three sizes too small. This was all the clothing I received as a P.O.W. They also gave us three blankets and a bowl of rice and some soup. We were then taken into the barracks, which consisted of individual cells approximately six feet long and ten feet wide with a barred window at the end. The floor was raised and a grass mat three by six feet was at one end. The three blankets and the grass mat were to be my bed for the next six months.

The camp was U-shaped, with the Japanese quarters in the middle and the barracks on each side. These were divided by a fence down the middle. The newer prisoners like myself were kept on one side and the older ones on the other. At first we were not even allowed to talk to each other, but later on we were allowed to talk to each other but not to the older prisoners.

We were not there very long when we were given a demonstration. They opened the gates that separated the two compounds and had the older prisoners line up facing the guards. Some prisoners were singled out for certain offences and were beaten with a club across the buttocks until they collapsed. After watching this I knew what could be expected if we didn't do what we were told.

In the beginning, we were each taken aside and interrogated. When it was my turn I was taken to a small room with a table and two chairs. A Japanese officer sat opposite me. He was very polite and could speak very good English. He would offer me a cigarette and ask me how everything was. He told me he had been educated in the U.S. He would ask me the same questions over and over as I would give him the same answers he would not accept. Then he let me leave. This happened only a few times. I guess he figured I didn't know anything.

The guards in this camp were very young and the ones that seemed to have some kind of education treated us halfway decent. The others you had to watch out for. It was winter and they would allow us to go out into the compound for exercise. The only clothing we had was what we had on our backs so they let us take a blanket with us. There we were all walking around in a circle with blankets over our heads looking like a bunch of Old Mother Hubbards. During this winter we experienced at least two feet of snow on the ground. There was not heat in the cells, in fact, you could see right through the cracks in the walls. So we talked the guards into letting several of us get together in one cell. This way the body heat would at least make it a little warmer. We would sit around in a circle and talk about food, food, food as our rations were getting smaller and smaller. We also discussed our personalities, and learned a lot about each other.

During this winter a young B-29 flier was shot down and brought to camp. He was badly wounded and soon died as our medical facilities were like nothing. I volunteered as one of the group that was to bury him, knowing that by doing this I would get a boiled potato as payment. We had to carry him some distance from the camp in deep snow to a hilly wooded area and then dig a hole. I will always remember this.

Because of the snow and the cold I don't think I had any feeling in my feet for about four months. We would stamp our feet and walk as much as possible to keep the circulation going. In the beginning, we were given a bath once a week, but that soon stopped. Boy did that bath feel good. We would wash up first with a small pan of water and soap, then climb into this large tub of real hot water and soak. This was the only time I could get feeling back into my feet.

Just before Christmas, we were given some Red Cross food boxes. This sure was a pleasant surprise. The boxes contained all sorts of things, including soap, cigarettes, gum, a chocolate bar, powdered milk, dried prunes or raisins, canned fish and meat, a small block of cheese, canned butter, and a can opener. This in turn created a little trading and the bartering would begin. Some wanted the chocolate bars, others wanted cigarettes, etc. Me, I kept just what I had and rationed it to myself accordingly. We received three boxes in all over a period of time. They had more but they would not give them to us. We figured that they wanted them for themselves.

Later, we were put over into the other compound as we were now considered the older prisoners as new ones were brought in. We heard that Pappy Boyington was in this camp and that he was assigned to the kitchen detail; therefore was able to obtain certain privileges. He would help us in every way he could.

One morning after our meal, we were all lined up in front of our barracks and accused of stealing some of the Red Cross food boxes that were stored at one end of the barracks. Of course, no one would admit to this crime, so we all had to stay at attention in front of the barracks until someone confessed. We stayed this way all day without eating. Come dinner time, there was still no confession, so they made us get into a pushup position. If anyone moved, a guard would hit them with a club across the buttocks. This didn't seem to work so they took us back inside the barracks and lined us up in the center and asked again who was responsible. Still no answer. Then the guards took turns and whacked us across the buttocks with a large club several times each. Still no answer, so they quit and gave us our dinner.

The very next morning we were transferred by train to our next camp, Omori, located on the shore of Tokyo Bay. Pappy Boyington was among us, so we sort of elected him to be in command of our little group. There were also some B-29 fliers with us and when we arrived at the camp we were all put together in one building and not allowed to see or talk with the other prisoners in the camp. We were kept like this as special prisoners all the time we were there.

The building I was in consisted of a dirt floor in the middle and raised wooden platforms on each side. On these wooden platforms is where I slept with the others. We all had diarrhea and I had developed berri-berri, so between the two, I wasn't in too good a shape. Our food by now consisted of a bucket of rice that was divided equally among us, half a cup each, along with a small bowl of soup three times a day. When I say rice, I mean it was a combination of barley, milamaze, and rice. Once in a while they would supplement the soup with a few pieces of dried fish. We never, ever, received any meat.

After we had been in this camp for some time, Boyington and the rest of us agreed we should be doing something with our time, so he talked the guards into letting us go out of the camp and plant vegetables in the bombed-out areas of the city. Every morning and afternoon, those that were well enough would be marched out of camp into the bombed-out areas and put to work.

We took along a five-gallon can of water for making tea to have at our breaks. Most of the time, I volunteered to be the tea tobin, the person responsible for making the tea. I remember one time we were near a fish market and one of us managed to slip away and obtain some fish. In turn, I boiled them in the pot of water that was for the tea. We intended on bringing them back to camp and having them with our evening meal. Unfortunately, it was discovered at the gate to the camp when we returned and was taken away. The leaders of our group, of course, were punished.

Also, while I was acting at tea tobin, I would wander away and scrounge around behind buildings that were still occupied and obtain choice bits of garbage like fish heads and pieces of vegetables. One time, when we were all on a tea break and sitting around talking, a stray old dog came around. We immediately discussed the possibility of eating this animal, but no one had the nerve to kill it.

I did everything possible to obtain extra food, so as the vegetables became ripe, I would pick them and eat them raw when the guard wasn't looking. When you're starving, anything tastes good besides your normal ration of soup and rice.

While in Omori, I experienced a large incendiary raid on the city of Yokohama. When the fireworks started, the Japanese boarded up all the windows in the barracks then went to the air-raid shelters. We were left exposed to the elements. It was frightening as bombs were dropping all around. Some fragments ended up in camp.

One morning we woke up and it was very quiet. There were no guards around! We realized something big was happening. We discovered only one guard in the whole camp. He told us the war was over, so we just took over the camp.

It was two weeks after this before our forces came and liberated us. During this time fighter planes and B-29 bombers flew over the camp and dropped tons of food and clothing. It got so bad this stuff was crashing through the building so we had to put a sign on the compound telling them to drop it outside of camp.

I was liberated two weeks after the end of hostilities and taken aboard the hospital ship *Benevolence*. I was put to bed and given blood and medication. I was also given a meal of bacon and eggs. When I was captured I weighed 170 pounds. Now I was down to about 100 pounds and I was in no condition to be flown home. Later, I was transferred to the hospital ship *Rescue*, which was returning to the States. It took twenty-one days but I didn't care. I knew I was going home! I arrived back in the States exactly two years after I left on October 25, 1943, and one year to the day our submarine was sunk October 25, 1944.

U.S. SUBMARINES IN THE PACIFIC

U.S. submarines did more damage to the Japanese war effort than any other class of ship. They accomplished in the Pacific what Germany's U-boats failed to do in the Atlantic.

But it was not easy. American torpedoes during the first years of the war were unreliable. Too many captains watched their torpedoes streak into a target only to bounce harmlessly off without exploding—and of course alerting the enemy to the presence and location of the American sub. Better torpedoes did not reach the Pacific until late in the war. Regardless, the U.S. Navy was able to strangle Japanese shipping efforts to the point that they could actually enter Tokyo Bay.

The Navy improved on German wolfpack tactics with coordination and precision never seen before. Surprisingly, the Japanese never mastered the escorted convoy practice that saved England in two World Wars.

The best torpedo in the war was the Japanese Long Lance. When launched from a torpedo assault aircraft, it was a devastating weapon. Japanese submarines were also equipped with the Long Lance but they never achieved the levels of success their enemies or allies could boast of.

I DIDN'T SEE A THING

by Walter C. Metz

In the Pacific, the Navy had a rotation plan. After eighteen months of sea duty, you were supposed to go back to the U.S.A. for rest and relaxation.

I was on a destroyer, the U.S.S. *Stembel*. We were on duty for twenty-four months before we were ordered home in August, 1945.

In July, 1945, we picked up some downed pilots and brought them back to their carrier. We went through the usual swap, we gave them back their pilots and they gave us two gallons of ice cream. Since we had no ice cream of our own, we thought we got the better of the deal.

The weather was stormy and as we pulled away from the carrier, the bow went into a wave and six of us on deck were knocked down. The water pushed me along the deck and I hit the starboard "bitts" used for tying up the ship lines. My right leg was broken in two places, the femur and the tibia. My five shipmates had assorted injuries.

On the destroyer, we had one doctor and a couple of pharmacist mates. Our sick bay was not equipped to tend our injuries. We were ordered to go alongside the U.S.S. *Alabama* and send our injured over to the battleship by breeches buoy. As they put my stretcher on the breeches buoy, someone said, as he pointed to a valve on my inflatable life jacket, "If the rope breaks pull this!" I closed my eyes as I left the *Stembel* and didn't open them until I heard someone on the *Alabama* say, "I got him."

I was taken below to sick bay where the doctor drilled a wire through my femur, put my leg in a splint, and attached a weight brace. This rig kept the leg from shrinking. (There is a picture of how I looked in this get up, on the bulkhead (wall) of sick bay on the *Alabama*). After a short stay, my five shipmates were sent back to the *Stembel,* and then back to the U.S.A. Since my injuries took longer to heal I stayed on the *Alabama* and continued my Pacific tour of duty.

I must say that I enjoyed my stay on the *Alabama*. All I did was lay in bed all day, had my meals served to me, and listened to the ship radio. What a life!

On the destroyer, when they sounded General Quarters, I'd start running to my battle station and pray "Dear God, I need you, please stay near me." On the *Alabama* when they sounded General Quarters I said "Thanks God for putting me on a battleship." I knew the Japs had nothing left that could sink the *Alabama*. I would just stay in bed and read a book.

In August, 1945, they dropped the bomb on Hiroshima and then on Nagasaki and it was all over. I remember Admiral Halsey saying on the ship radio, "Men, the war is over. Well done. Japan is no longer our enemy. Should any Japanese planes approach the task force, you will shoot them down in friendly fashion."

September 2, 1945, the *Alabama* was in Tokyo Bay for the surrender ceremonies. I saw nothing from my bed. We went to Hawaii and then headed for the U.S.A.

People lined up on the Golden Gate Bridge, as the Fleet steamed into San Francisco Bay. Signs all over said "Welcome Home!" They even had one on Alcatraz!

The crew told me it was a very emotional greeting. A few sailors said "If they had the papers handy, they would have re-enlisted." But I saw nothing from my bed.

On the way back from Hawaii, the doctor pulled the wire out of my leg. He may have taken it out too soon. One day I got my toe caught in my bed sheet, when I pulled my leg to free it, the femur bent. It looked like I had two knees.

When the *Alabama* anchored in San Francisco Bay, they took me out of bed and up to the main deck. The first thing I saw was the sunlight and the Bay Bridge. What a sight! I'm home! At Treasure Island Naval Hospital they had to break my leg again and put a silver plate in my leg. But who cares, I'm home and I can see things!

FIGHTING THE KOREAN WAR
AT LUKE AIR FORCE BASE
by Ken Tomb

In the spring of 1950 life was about as good as it gets for a young man in Uncle Sam's Air Force. I had the good fortune to be stationed at Williams Air Force Base in Arizona where the workload was light, promotions came quickly, and there was more time off than most of us could afford.

About fifty air miles to the west, Luke Air Force Base had been closed since the end of World War II and its only occupant was the newly formed unit of the Arizona Air National Guard, the 197th Fighter Squadron. The Guard possessed a motley collection of aircraft including a C-47, a couple of B-26s, and a handful of F-51 Mustangs. Like most Guard units during this period they were virtually ignored by the Air Force and free to fly anywhere, anytime they wanted to and get paid for doing it. Life for them was also very good.

Unfortunately, this carefree existence came to an end on June 25, 1950, when the North Korean army crossed the 38th parallel and invaded their neighbors to the south, beginning what was euphemistically called the "Korean Police Action." Flying hours quickly doubled and then tripled at Williams. Prior to this there had been only one class of cadets in training at any given time, now there would be at least three. This increase in activity was quickly assimilated as the troops at "Willy" rose to the challenge.

At Luke, however, it was a different situation. The changes that the Guardsmen had to make were next to overwhelming. Not only was that happy band of weekend warriors ordered to active duty, they were given the task of reopening the base and making it operational as quickly as possible. Luke had fallen on hard times since World War II, and except for the few buildings the Guard unit occupied, it was abandoned and allowed to deteriorate to the point where it was practically untenable. Not only had nature taken its toll, but most of the transplantable landscaping and almost anything else of value had been removed and shipped across the valley to Williams. Had the Guard unit not been there it might have taken up to a year to bring the base to a point where it could be utilized and the war effort in Korea would have been seriously handicapped—at least as far as air support was concerned.

GUARD DUTY

If all this wasn't enough, the guardsmen then suffered the cruelest blow of all. Their reliable old F-51 Mustangs were taken away and replaced by a squadron of the most unreliable and difficult to maintain aircraft ever built: the early model Republic F-84B/C Thunderjet. This aircraft had already been proven inadequate for what it was designed to do, and would have been dropped from the inventory had the war in Korea not shown how woefully unequipped and unprepared the Air Force was for any sustained military action. Most of the F-51s reclaimed from the Guard

Squadrons were sent to the combat zone to be utilized in air to ground support, a role they were not ideally suited for. The aircraft that was most effective in this type of action was the Republic F-47 Thunderbolt, and they had long since been sent to the smelters or given to some third world country. This situation would be repeated twenty years later when we had to buy back Douglas ADs from the French to fight the war in Indo-China.

It was at this point that my life also took a turn for the worse. Since the maintenance folks in the Guard had no previous experience with jet aircraft it was decided that some of us so called "old hands" would be transferred to Luke in April of 1951, and we received the princely sum of $1.72 in travel funds, the price of a bus ticket. Leaving Williams was not something I wanted to do but with only three months of my enlistment left I wasn't overly concerned.

The reassignment seemed like a reasonable idea at the time, but it was not to be a happy arrangement, because the relationship between the regular Air Force and the National Guard was strained at best. The Air Force considered the Guard to be a group of amateurs playing soldier and the Guard resented the contemptuous attitude of the Air Force personnel and thought them to be arrogant and overrated. These arguments had some basis in truth, but they were not conducive to a cooperative effort. In my case, the Guard people thought that the only benefit to be gained from my presence was to relieve them of a lot of unpleasant duties. As a result of my three stripes, I had not had any of these duties for some time, but the First Sergeant unhesitatingly assigned me to K.P. as soon as I got there, and from then on our relationship went downhill. As far as the maintenance knowledge I was able to impart; that too proved to be less than desired. I had never seen an F-84 and the experience I had with T-33s and F-80s did not lend itself to maintaining the troublesome reject from Republic Aviation.

About this time, the Arizona unit was joined by two squadrons from the Michigan Air Guard and a squadron of F-51s from Nellis Air Force Base in Nevada. These units were combined to form the 127th Pilot Training Wing, which made the distinction between Guard and regular Air Force less apparent. After a short period of forced cohabitation the people at Luke Air Force Base got down to the business of training fighter pilots for the war in Korea.

With little regard for my lack of supervisory experience I was given the temporary assignment of Flight Chief and after a short and inadequate familiarization period, was placed in charge of six very intimidating F-84Cs and a group of young men who were even less prepared for this adventure than I was—a sure-fire recipe for disaster if there ever was one. Nowhere else would a three striper have had this responsibility, but as the saying goes, "In the land of the blind a one-eyed man is king." It was only by the grace of God and certainly through no ability of mine that we never lost an airplane from my flight. Unfortunately, the same could not be said for the rest of the base.

The three F-84 squadrons proceeded to compile the highest loss rate of any non-combat unit in the history of the Air Force. No less than two dozen aircraft were lost during this period, most of them resulting in fatalities. And the accident rate was equally as bad on the ground. A number of maintenance men were injured, some fatally due to their lack of experience, and as far as I know this record still stands. I don't know of another set of circumstances that could have led to this type of situation. Moreover, such an appalling safety record would simply not be tolerated in today's Air Force. The training and safety procedures in place now eliminate the likelihood of that sort of thing ever happening again. But at the time, it was accepted as an unavoidable risk and considering the conditions that brought it about, that was probably true. There was no other choice but to use aircraft that were unsafe and personnel who were untrained because there were simply no others available.

First and foremost among the causes of this unenviable record was the unsuitability of the F-84B/C. Being overweight and underpowered, it definitely was not an aircraft to be flown by inexperienced pilots from runways with surface temperatures that regularly exceeded 150 degrees as they did in the summertime in Arizona. And it certainly was not an aircraft that could be safely maintained by untrained mechanics. The operating systems were loaded with maintenance problems that only well-trained and equipped technicians could properly cope with. This was a seriously flawed aircraft that had been recommended for limited use almost as soon as it came off the assembly line. Some pilots actually enjoyed flying the old F-84 because it was such a stable gun platform (once you got it in the air). But I suspect their enjoyment would have been limited had they known what a risky proposition it was to fly this beast. I have always felt that combat must have been a bit easier for them after training at Luke because in Korea the odds of surviving were much better. Fortunately, there were none of the old F-84s in Korea and later versions, namely the "E" and "G" models, contributed a large share of the "Air to Ground" war and proved to be very successful aircraft that went on to serve the Air Force for many years without the problems the early models encountered.

In a strange way, it was this lack of serviceability that may have prevented even more lives being lost because if the in-commission rate had been higher, the accident rate would probably have increased proportionally. I recall one memorable morning when the entire 127th Pilot Training wing could not produce a single flyable F-84. Later on, as we gained experience, things improved somewhat and thirty hours logged by one aircraft in a month was considered so outstanding that the crew chief was given a three-day pass and an engraved cigarette lighter for his achievement, but this was an exception not to be repeated for some time.

Not all the problems were due to poor maintenance, however. There were not enough spare parts to keep up with the demand. I suspect this was because no one thought the aircraft would be around long enough to require a back log of parts. Cannibalization became the norm and eventually there were more aircraft AOCP (Aircraft Out of Commission for Parts) than there were in commission. Our maintenance officer and a few carefully selected personnel actually made a midnight raid on a supply depot and spirited away a few engine tailcones in order to relieve the situation. Like a plot from a movie, a couple of them distracted the supply personnel while the rest went over the fence and got the tailcones. They made their getaway in a C-47 and brought the booty back to Luke in a valiant but misguided effort to raise the in-commission rate. They succeeded in their effort but were severely reprimanded when their dirty deed was discovered. The Guard troops may have been short on maintenance experience, but they had other talents that they excelled at.

Another contributing factor in the poor performance at Luke was the low morale of the troops. We were poorly equipped, the chow was bad, the base was run down and barely habitable, and there was never anything to show for all the effort being put forth. There were few, if any, that would not have welcomed a transfer to Korea, but getting out of the training command at that time was next to impossible. The base commander during this period was a gentleman who could charitably be called eccentric. In his way he tried to improve the situation, but like the rest of us, he was unprepared for the task that confronted him. He had been a fighter pilot in the CBI theater during the war and had a couple victories to his credit, but as a leader of men he left a lot to be desired. One of his more memorable efforts to create what he called "Luke Air Park" was to have the buildings painted in various shades of blue, green, yellow, and pink. He also decreed that we should wear short pants and bush jackets in order to improve our image. You can imagine how this went over with the troops working on the aircraft in the hot sun. I suppose he meant well, but the answer to the problems at Luke was not pink barracks and short pants. His strange personality and sometimes bizarre behavior will long be remembered by those of us who were under his command.

Due to the high attrition rate of the F-84s, the three squadrons were soon condensed into two. It's hard to believe but we had lost the equivalent of one whole squadron of airplanes. In retrospect, it seems almost criminal to have expected pilots to train under such conditions. But we didn't know any better and even if we had it wouldn't have made any difference because there was no other choice than to work with what was available. After the realignment of the group, to my great delight, my Squadron was re-equipped with F-80s and I was relieved of my temporary duties as flight chief. I then resumed my old and familiar role as a T-33 crew chief. This was one of my happier moments at Luke, but this happiness was tempered by the fact that my enlistment had been extended a year. I could understand the reason for the extension, but I only had two weeks to go when it happened and that did not go down easily.

As it turned out, the year's extension that I received was one of the most fortuitous events in my life. In January of 1952, after assuring my commanding officer that I fully intended to make the Air Force my career (a lie that I have never regretted), I was promoted to staff sergeant. It was also during this year that I became well acquainted with a number of the former National Guard members, and these friendships would have a great deal of influence in what did turn out to be my life's work, a career in the Air National Guard that would last for the next thirty-four years.

TAKING CARE OF THEIR OWN

by Tom Griggs

M arines take care of their own. Our drill instructor told us that in boot camp, and I saw a good example in 1968 in Vietnam.

My reconnaissance team stumbled into a North Vietnamese Army battalion command post in the mountains southwest of Hue. Luckily for us, most of the NVA soldiers were preparing to ambush a Marine convoy on Vietnam's Highway 1, so were not home. However, plenty of enemy soldiers remained behind at the large camp, and we ended up engaged in a heavy firefight with them.

We were outnumbered and outgunned, but soon two Huey gunships and two attack jets arrived to help us. Amazingly, the only enemy round to find its target was an AK-47 round that ripped through my plastic canteen. The senior Huey pilot quickly determined our location and the enemy positions, and the two choppers went to work with their 2.75-inch rockets and machine guns, briefly silencing the North Vietnamese.

Meanwhile, we scrambled over the top of a ridgeline, so the jets could put some 250-pound bombs on top of the enemy, but not take us out at the same time. The fixed wing aircraft screeched down from above, and the impacting bombs shook the whole ridgeline. We bounced up and down like rubber balls. Shrapnel tore through the tree branches above us. Amidst the thunderous devastation around us, we escaped.

Darkness arrived as we crawled into the thickest brush we could find. I asked the Huey pilot, a Marine major, how long he'd be in the area. He said he'd stick around as long as we wanted, but he was low on fuel. I told him to go home, and we would sit tight. The major said he would return in the morning.

At first light, we heard the sound of two gunships approaching.

The major was back. He radioed us, telling me he found an opening in the mountian forest big enough for a chopper to land. With that, we crawled out of the brush, put on our gear and simply followed the slow-flying major to the jungle opening, where we were picked up. Marines do take care of their own.

A BAD PLACE TO VISIT
AND A WORSE PLACE TO LIVE
by B. Wilder Merrill

C amau is in the Mekong Delta at the extreme southern end of
Vietnam. This low-land region is hot, flat, humid, and has the
indescribable smell of Southeast Asia. It's covered by rice paddies
and thousands of interlocking canals. Most of its people are simple,
peasant rice-farmers, who move their commerce by small boats
called sampans.

In the best of times, Camau wouldn't be a good place to visit.
During 1963 it was a bad place to visit and a worse place to live. The
Viet Cong were infiltrating this rice bowl for its vast food supply,
while waging a campaign of terror, including theft, torture, forced
taxation, kidnap, and murder.

Beginning in late 1961, U.S. Advisors were sent to Vietnam and
by 1963, there were about 16,000 advisors in the country to help
stem the communist insurgency. Some advisors not only advised but
took part in combat operations. Among those who did were Capt.
Earl C. Meek and S. Sgts. Bernard W. Merrill and Joseph Lesch, U.S.
Air Force. They were part of an Explosive Ordnance Disposal (EOD)
Team, whose mission was to helicopter into contested areas to blow
up shot-down U.S. aircraft. This, in turn, denied the VC from capturing aircraft bombs, rockets, ammunition, and machine guns.

During this early phase of the war—the VC called it a People's
War—the VC were short of arms and munitions. Therefore, they
used captured ordnance to make improvised mines and booby traps.
Moreover, they employed captured aircraft cannons and machine
guns as ground weapons. The VC were masters at improvising captured ordnance and making "backyard" munitions of their own.

South Vietnam was an EOD man's nightmare—unexploded
ordnance was strewn from one end of the country to the other!
Much of the ordnance was from France, Japan, Russia, Red China,

North Korea, North Vietnam, and the United States. This ordnance was a deadly reminder of South Vietnam's violent history of foreign occupation, civil war, and the communist insurgency sponsored by North Vietnam's National Liberation Front.

On September 11, 1963, headquarters at Tan Son Nhut Air Base, Saigon, alerted Captain Meek for a counterinsurgency (COIN) mission. VC ground fire had hit a U.S. trainer-fighter plane, forcing its pilot to crash-land. He pancaked the plane with its bombs and rockets intact. The pilot was rescued in the Camau Peninsula, where there was no friendly defense perimeter.

Meek, Merrill, and Lesch packed their gear and flew by Carabou (transport plane) to Camau's main airstrip. From there they flew in a Vietnamese Air Force Huey helicopter to a spit of land hardly big enough to land on. The EOD team debarked and the helicopter took off quickly—apparently its crew wanted no part of VC country.

It was noon and already the heat and humidity were in the high 80s. The shotdown plane was visible in a rice paddy at about 400 meters. Meek, Merrill, and Lesch—armed with .45 caliber pistols, automatic carbines, and haversacks of composition C-4 plastic explosive—sloshed through the stagnant paddy water.

They reached the plane which was slightly nosed over in about one meter of water. They started placing C-4 explosive charges on the plane's fuel cells, machine guns, 250-pound bombs, and rocket pods, which contained 2.75 folding-fin aircraft rockets.

Unexpectedly, a pitched battle began about 400 meters away between a VC infantry unit and an Army of the Republic of Vietnam (ARVN) unit. The racket was deafening: rifles and automatic weapons were shooting, while grenades, ground-fired rockets, and mortar rounds were detonating. The EOD troops saw heavy cordite smoke, muzzle flashes, and the faint red streaks that tracer rounds make during daylight.

Suddenly, four U.S. B-26 light bombers (rehabs from World War II) screeched in low, firing high-explosive rockets and .50 caliber machine guns at the VC's left flank. Some of the rockets and machine gun rounds hit only about 100 meters from Meek, Merrill, and Lesch.

Then Meek hollered, "Take cover!" He, Merrill, and Lesch crouched low in the water behind the plane, while a VC machine gun punched dozens of slugs through the plane and surrounding water. Incredibly, none of the three was hit.

The incoming rounds stopped. They got up and used parts of the plane as a bench rest for their carbines. Then they slid their rear sight ramps to the maximum 300-yard elevation, because the VC were 400 meters away. Using "Kentucky windage" to increase elevation, they each fired short bursts of automatic fire toward the VC's left flank. After each fired two twenty-round magazines, they took cover and watched the fire fights.

No fire was returned, so Meek climbed up on the plane's left wing to pack a machine gun with C-4. Meanwhile, Merrill and Lesch were stringing and tying detonation cord to charges on the plane's right side.

The slug seemed to come from nowhere. It hit Meek's right front thigh, blowing out about seven inches of bone through the back of his leg. He screamed, "Oh, my God!" The impact knocked him from the plane's wing into the water flat on his back.

Merrill rushed behind Meek, grabbed him under the armpits, and pulled his head and shoulders above water to prevent his drowning. Lesch got to Meek's front and tried to place a tourniquet from his snake-bite kit above the horrible wound. But Meek's thigh was so swollen it split his pant leg, and the tourniquet was too short to fit around his thigh.

Strands of detonation cord were still hanging from Merrill's neck, so he gave Lesch a length of it to use as a tourniquet. It worked: Lesch placed it above the wound and tightened it with a pair of blasting cap crimpers. The gushing blood stopped. Remarkably, Meek was still conscious.

By pure luck, there was an abandoned sampan nearby about the size of a row boat. It listed and was weather-worn, but buoyant enough to float and carry weight. Merrill and Lesch carried Meek—who was six foot three and weighed 210 pounds—and rolled him into the sampan. It took twenty or thirty minutes, about half of the way under fire, to push Meek to the spot of land on which they had originally landed. (On dry, level land, it would have been a five-minute walk.)

Just before reaching land, Merrill ignited a red smoke grenade hoping to attract a "dust off" (medical evacuation helicopter or "medevac"). Soon a light U.S. artillery spotter plane swooped down to about thirty feet and threw out a canvas cartridge belt; it landed in the water close to Merrill. He retrieved it and found a handwritten note in one of its pockets. It said "We know you have wounded—dust off on way." (Merrill thought that even if Meek did make it, he would probably never meet the spotter pilot to thank him.)

Only fifteen minutes passed, but they seemed infinite. Then a U.S. Army dust-off chopper landed. It was newly painted with brown-green camouflage and big, bright red crosses, which made it look odd—but certainly welcomed. Two medics—who looked like real pros—jumped out carrying a gurney. One had a .38 revolver sticking out of his waistband. The other wore a .45 pistol in a shoulder rig and both wore cloth Combat Medical badges.

They loaded Meek into the chopper. One medic was already plugging a bottle of glucose into him. Merrill and Lesch threw Meek's carbine and haversack into the chopper after him.

It was unbelievable: Meek, with a wound large enough to put a beer can into it sideways, was still conscious. So much so, that he told Merrill to take Lesch and go back and blow up the plane! Then the dust-off revved off to Camau.

Merrill and Lesch were exhausted, but being pissed off at the VC did wonders to their adrenaline. They decided to use the sampan to lean on as a "walker" and for cover against small-arms fire. Before leaving, they checked each other's haversack for fuse lighters, time fuse, detonating cord, blasting-cap crimpers, a wooden box of #10 blasting caps, and two blocks of composition C-4.

Staggering and crouching low, they pushed the sampan from its aft end. About midway to the plane, four dead VC in black pajamas were floating face down. Caution told Merrill to cover the risk of any VC being alive. Consequently, he shot a carbine round into each one's head. The impact popped their heads underwater, and they bobbed up like four pop-up targets.

The VC and Government of Vietnam (GVN) troops were still engaged in a series of furious firefights—punctuated by pops, booms, muzzle flashes and, semi- and automatic-weapons fire. But now, the VC were being slowly routed toward the downed plane. It appeared, however, that Merrill and Lesch could beat them in a foot race to the plane and demolish it.

They ditched the sampan and ran splashing to the plane. Merrill primed the remaining machine gun and rocket pod with C-4, while

Lesch made a dual fusing system to insure detonation. He crimped a blasting cap on each of two lengths of time fuse. Then he bent three-inch U shapes on the two detonation cord leads, and taped in the two blasting caps. Merrill and Lesch each pushed on a fuse lighter, pulled the fuse-lighter strikers, and hauled ass toward the spot of land.

They got about 150 meters when they saw the red-orange flash, which turned into a huge fireball. The explosion was extraordinary due to the chemical explosion of the C-4 and ordnance, which combine with the mechanical explosion of air and gas in the aircraft's fuel cells. The boom was much louder than normal because of the low cloud cover and humid, thick atmosphere.

Merrill and Lesch ducked underwater, as fragments from the ordnance and plane flew everywhere. A few seconds later they stood up. Lesch looked at Merrill and said, "That was a hell of a shot! Did any VC get hit?"

Merrill replied, "I can't tell, Joe. But I'm sure a lot of them shit in their black pajamas!"

After dark, Merrill and Lesch were extracted by a U.S. Army Huey and flown to Camua. They spent the night in an Army barracks, where they ate and showered. But they had to wear their same fatigues, which smelled of cordite and were covered with mud, sweat, and Meek's blood.

The next morning they flew to Tan Son Nhut in Saigon, where they were met by the other three members of the EOD team. They related that Meek had passed through the day before and was given nineteen pints of whole blood—three of which were from the EOD members. He was then flown up to a field hospital in Danang, I Corps.

Merrill and Lesch caught a flight to Danang a few days later to visit Meek. He lay on a cot in a hospital tent drinking a can of soda; he said the doctor advised a lot of liquid. A pillow was where his right leg should have been. He explained that an arterial transplant had been attempted to save his leg. However, his temperature shot so high that his leg had to be amputated to save his life.

Meek was in good spirits considering what he had gone through. But two things concerned him: He wanted to remain in service, and wanted to walk with a prosthesis before seeing his wife and daughter in the States. But both wants proved to be unfulfilled.

Upon leaving Meek, Merrill and Lesch met the surgeon, an Army

Major, who had operated on Meek. He said that Meek would soon transfer to the Philippines for a while, and then go Stateside to recuperate.

Within a few months, Merrill and Lesch finished their tours and returned to the "land of the big PX." Several months later, Meek was awarded the Bronze Star with Combat V for valor and the Purple Heart, and Merrill and Lesch were also awarded Bronze Stars. Merrill retired in 1968 and served in Vietnam again during 1969 and 1970—this time in the Central Intelligence Agency.

To Merrill's knowledge, neither he, Meek, nor Lesch has seen one another since 1963 in Vietnam. However, Merrill retains a 1964 letter from Meek. Here it is verbatim:

☆ ☆ ☆ 20 April, 1964 ☆ ☆ ☆

Dear Sergeant Merrill,

Thanks for your letter of 28 March, which just arrived via Utah, Vietnam, and San Diego. I'm sorry I haven't written sooner, but there seemed to be so many things to occupy my time recently. Unfortunately, I'm not PCS to Hill Air Force Base. I'm still in the hospital here, and will be for the next few months. We're still encountering difficulties trying to fit my stump with a new leg, which won't irritate the extensive scar tissue on the back of my leg. Because of the serious infection which I had, the doctors are hesitant to operate for a revision. Apparently, the infection has not disappeared, but still remains, though dormant. I'm hoping that things will be completely under control in another three months or so.

It is my understanding that I will be unable to remain on active duty, however this decision is by no means definite. I have a few plans to assist me which I haven't augmented yet, but it appears it will be necessary to do so.

I finally learned that both you and Lesch were awarded the Bronze Star for your heroism on September 11th. Frankly, I feel you both deserve the Medal of Honor for saving my life. Colonel Walker assured me that both of you would be recognized for your performance that day, but I'm saddened to learn that your decorations weren't more appropriate to the occasion.

I have my family located in San Francisco, and I'm able to spend the weekends with them. This helps break up the hospital routine very nicely, and of course, I enjoy being with my wife and daughter again.

I appreciated hearing from you, and I'm certain you realize I shall be forever grateful to you for your assistance to me. If I can ever be of assistance to you, I would consider it a pleasure if you would call on me.

My very best wishes to you.

Warmest regards,
Signed/Earl Meek

No doubt about it—a few hours in Camau changed Meek's whole life. Yet time can be anomalous: Peasant farmers still move their rice in sampans over the low lands. And Camau's smell is still indescribable.

CORPSMAN
by Robert C. Hubbard

I was a nineteen-year-old medical corpsman, assigned to the Second Platoon, Lima Company, Third Battalion, Fourth Marines, Third Marine Division. We operated mainly near the Demilitarized Zone. Our job was to try to prevent the North Vietnamese Army from crossing the border into South Vietnam.

☆ ☆ ☆ The Ambush ☆ ☆ ☆
(June 29-July 15, 1967)

On the evening of my first ambush we had about twelve to fifteen men including an M-60 team. We left the relative safety of our perimeter at dusk and went down a well-worn dirt road at a slow pace, weapons on semi-automatic. With about fifteen meters between each man, in a staggered column, it was just dark enough to make it difficult to catch a glimpse of the man in front of you. Being so new to the 'Nam, Corporal Bruckner, the big, African-American squad leader, told me to stay in the middle of the column and keep my eyes open.

We walked about 1,000 meters out and stopped; everyone down on one knee with every other man facing outboard. On one side of the road was an open field. On the other side was a ridge about three feet high. We moved off the road and into the ridge bank with our backs against it facing the open flank across the road. The elephant grass was waist-high and razor sharp. We set in against the ridge bank with the gun team marching in the middle. We had two men above and on top of the ridge bank, both facing behind us, for rear security.

I was placed on the right side of the M-60 team between the ammo humper and the radio operator. We were all settled in when Corporal Bruckner whispered on down the line, "Every man awake until 2400 hours then every other man sleeps two hours in rotation. If you spot any movement, fire a pom-pom and open up." That sounded good to me but if we heard or saw movement why couldn't we fire first then send up a flare? How green I was! (I would learn in time.)

What seemed like only minutes later we heard a "WHOOSH." I had been sitting up Indian-style when I heard that sound. Then I fell backwards thinking it was incoming mortars, artillery, or rockets. All of a sudden the night turned into day. Someone had fired a pom-pom and all the men were laying down a base of fire. Private First Class Sames told me to fire so I squeezed off a few rounds into the area across the road. Even with the sky lit up by the illumination from the pom-poms.

I couldn't see the enemy and there didn't appear to be any return fire. Corporal Bruckner raised his voice above the firing. "Let's go!" he yelled.

"Where're we going?" I yelled to no one in particular over the din of the firing.

I really didn't want to go charging through the elephant grass toward the unknown enemy, especially since the pom-pom flares had burned out after floating to the ground.

There was no semblance to a column as we briskly jogged back to our perimeter with the rear security man firing out into the darkness at unseen enemy targets. Lieutenant Adams met our squad as we reached the outer perimeter. "Jesus Christ. What the hell happened out there?" he yelled.

"The gun team spotted movement so we threw up a flare, opened up and got out," replied Bruckner.

We were then ordered to do an about-face and go back out, setting up in a new location and put the ambush back in operation. Taking all this in I kept hearing "Shit," and other choice objections to our new orders. We went back out, being very careful not to set up in the same vicinity, and remained there for the rest of the night.

Sames informed me that they did this type of charade quite a lot. Set up an ambush, wait a few minutes, pop a flare, open up with their weapons and run back into the perimeter where they could usually get a good night's sleep. But lately, Lieutenant Adams had been getting wise to their actions. So, for the remainder of the night, I slept on and off while taking my turn on radio watch, which was the communications link with the other squads, CP and Lima Company. (No enemy contact was made for the rest of the night.)

☆ ☆ ☆ Sick Call ☆ ☆ ☆

Our platoon wasn't scheduled for any patrols or ambushes that day or the next. Doc Hortez spent a lot of time going over the various medications and treatments used in the field. We held sick call later that evening with several men coming over to us with horrible looking feet due to the wet conditions of the Vietnam climate. "Dumb ass. Take your boots off once in a while and change your socks," Chico would say to them. "Wet feet like these can lead to immersion foot and a trip back to the BAS (Battle Aid Station) in the rear making us look bad in preventive medicine plus this would cut down on platoon strength in numbers," he'd say to me. He used to preach that good preventive medicine was the key to combating infection.

One patient who came to us was covered from head to foot with ugly red sores or pustules scabbed over and filled with superative material better known as pus. This was my first look at Private First Class Barker and his chronic condition known as jungle rot. Chico had me administer a penicillin injection in each buttock then coat the larger sores with bacitracin ointment after having first scrubbed off the foul-smelling, crusty scabs and draining the pus from them. His face, arms, and hands were the most affected although he did have some jungle rot on his legs. This treatment proved somewhat effective but was not long-lasting. Barker was to become a steady patient for my remaining time in the 'Nam.

Besides treating jungle rot we, as corpsmen, encountered the usual headaches, toothaches, sunburns, pulled muscles, and other assorted maladies. Also encountered were numerous types of stomach upsets and various types of dysentery problems. We treated these as best we could with what we had on hand and at our disposal. Otherwise, if the problem became too severe, we would have to send the sick or injured Marine back to the BAS for more definitive treatment with medications we just didn't have out in the field. We could just carry only so much gear.

Besides going out on patrols and ambushes we held sick call daily and stood radio watch during the night for two hours. We split the watch with other members of the platoon while the others slept, were on security watch, or out on listening post duty. I usually ended up getting the 12:00 P.M. to 2:00 A.M. watch or, the worst of them all, the 2:00 A.M. to 4:00 A.M. watch. We caught our sleep when and where we could whether it was on the ground or in a foxhole. We learned how to catch a few winks even when the monsoon rains were pelting us for days and nights on end.

When your radio watch ended you had to try and wake up the man who had the next watch and that was sometimes quite hard to do. No one wanted to be roused from a semi-sound sleep just to stay awake for two hours making radio checks with the Lima Company Command Post.

One day we were issued two cans of warm beer per man and even though they were warm they sure tasted fantastic. Wondering why everyone began bitching and moaning when the beer was handed out, I asked Sergeant Allen, who told me the reason. "When we get beer or soda rations it means we'll be going back out into the bush." The beer and soda were building us up for the news of an impending mission.

During the next several days we lost some men due to the rotation system and we were issued new ammo, grenades and stocked up on chow. I learned how to carry several days' supply of chow in a well-stretched sock by tying it on the back of my flak jacket through the armholes. This prevented the clinking and clanging of C-ration tin against tin. At least it helped muffle the sound.

Doc Hortez gave me a small notebook which was used to hold the names of all the men in the platoon, their squad designation, blood types and the last four digits of their service numbers. This would aid me in writing out medevac tags on dead or wounded Marines.

I didn't look forward to that very unpleasant task. Chico told me of a firefight he had been in some months earlier; a bad one. He hadn't had time to write out any medevac tags at all. I was secretly hoping I could respond to a situation like that and live to tell about it. I would do my best. It would have been okay with me if I never had to unwrap and open a field dressing or push some young Marine's intestines back into his abdominal cavity.

☆ ☆ ☆ First Casualty ☆ ☆ ☆
(July 15-July 25, 1967)

It was mid-July and Lima Company moved out to patrol the outer perimeter of Camp Carroll. We had been transported by convoy trucks several miles outside the perimeter and proceeded by foot some five miles further. Our artillery was always on-call whenever we had to use it to help us out. Grid coordinates were known in advance just in case! On company maneuvers such as this we had our own detachment of 60 mm. mortars.

Out in the bush we would set up in a loose perimeter with the CP in the middle and operate from it running patrols daily and ambushes nightly for two or three days, then move to another area and begin the cycle all over again. The patrols and ambushes proved uneventful except on one day when it was my turn to go out on a squad patrol.

Sergeant Raymond was the squad leader as we slowly made our way across an open area at the edge of a tree line. We soon came upon a non-detonated VC or NVA mortar round. It wasn't embedded in the ground so Raymond figured an enemy soldier had dropped or discarded it feeling it added too much weight to his load. Or maybe it was booby-trapped!

The rest of the squad formed a loose perimeter for defensive purposes while I knelt by the tree line allowing Raymond to look the round over. Facing outboard there came an explosion from the center of the perimeter. As usual, I thought we were being mortared. Then I heard a yell which would become all too familiar in the months ahead. "Corpsman up!" Grabbing my Unit 1, I ran from the tree line to where Raymond was lying on the ground clutching his thigh. As I reached him I saw that somehow the round had detonated, sending a piece of hot, jagged metal into his upper thigh. By this time the men knew it had been booby-trapped so they tightened up their defensive perimeter for possible action.

Sergeant Raymond threw his arm around my neck and we hobbled over to the tree line which would offer some form of concealment while I administered to his wound. (An open area was no place to perform medical aid unless the wounded man was in critical condition or we were pinned down.)

Wrapping a field dressing around the wound, while checking for a portal of exit, I glanced at his pupils and checked his pulse and pallor for any signs of shock. Observing none, I continued to dress his wound. It didn't appear too deep and luckily the femoral artery and its accompanying vein had been spared.

Anyone who sustains a traumatic wound such as this naturally has a feeling of apprehension but Raymond was holding up well. He would require a medevac although not on an emergency priority basis. The other squad members would have time to scout the area making sure the enemy wasn't nearby. Otherwise, we would have to change our location so the medevac chopper could come in to a secure landing zone as the round could have been electronically detonated by some VC or NVA waiting in the bushes for us to come along.

While filling out the medevac tag, and checking Raymond's pulse again, there was a call of, "Doc, over here!" Another Marine,

Lieutenant Corporal Jason had been hit in the thigh also, by flying shrapnel, but hadn't realized it until now. The flow of blood from his superficial wound was minimal, although the hot, searing metal would have to be excised by the surgeon back at the Battalion Aid Station. Bandaging the second casualty I felt my first encounter with the enemy, unseen as he was, had been handled quite professionally. As I completed the second medevac tag the chopper made its way into a secure landing zone. Raymond and Jason would be out of the shit; for a little while, at least.

As we made our way back into the company perimeter I was greeted with, "Good going, Doc" and "You're not a cherry boy, now, Doc." I had not realized that the entire Lima Company had monitored our call for a medevac dust-off for our two WIAs at the designated coordinates. It made me feel good inside knowing I had been accepted into the combat veterans fraternity by my comrades. I felt relieved that the two casualties were not seriously wounded and that they both would be back with us shortly. My baptism was over but at their expense.

☆ ☆ ☆   The Extraction   ☆ ☆ ☆

It was late July when I realized my twentieth birthday was fast approaching on July 30th. I was feeling older and somewhat wiser; at least in the day-to-day life in the bush. Most of the Marines were in their late teens and early twenties with the exception of Lieutenant Adams, Staff Sergeant Allen, and Sergeant Raymond.

On July 29th we were told to saddle-up, draw 300 rounds of ammo per man, and grab some extra C-rations. Apparently, a company from the Ninth Marines was taking a severe beating from the combined efforts of many VC and NVA some miles below the DMZ, also known as the buffer zone, strip, or trace. Our Lima Company was to act as a reactionary-blocking force while the Ninth pulled back to regroup and evacuate their casualties. I was really nervous and uptight about this operation. Why, I didn't know. Something just didn't feel right to me.

It was something to behold. Marine tanks were pulling back from the bamboo forest piled high with dead and wounded men. The walking- wounded had to do just that while following the tanks. The LZ was still hot and the canopy overhead was too thick for Huey gunships and medevac choppers to penetrate.

This pullback was the only sensible thing to do.

We were to cover the extraction but enemy opposition was light with only sporadic gunfire from some remaining snipers. We were much better off than the Ninth as they had taken many casualties during their engagement with the enemy. We dug in for the night anticipating an assault to completely wipe us out while we acted as a blocking force between the enemy and the remainder of the Ninth Marines. The victory which the VC-NVA had just won would go to their heads and, while the momentary victory belonged to them, they would probably try to add another triumph to their credit by assaulting our positions this night. To make matters worse, Lieutenant Adams had volunteered one of our squads to go out and set up an ambush! We all knew the enemy was still out there just waiting. We had seen the evidence of their presence.

This sounded like a suicide mission to me but it was my turn to go out with the squad and did so but with much trepidation. Lieutenant Adams led us out and we were all nervous and on edge. We wandered out of the makeshift safety of our perimeter in a staggered column and couldn't see shit! It was dark as death with no illumination from the moon.

We had gone about 500 meters or so and were preparing to set in when Private First Class Damos, a short-timer and the M-60 machine gun team leader, cut loose with a burst from his gun. I could see the red tracers, every fifth round, making their way out into the hot, dark night as I hit the ground. Lieutenant Adams was furious. "What'd you do, Damos, hit one of our own men?" "No sir, Lieutenant," replied little Damos. "I saw something in the hedgerow." Bless his ass. We never knew if he actually saw anything but we gladly left our ambush site as we now had compromised our ambush position, and returned to our blocking-reactionary force perimeter.

Soaked with sweat I was glad to be back with the rest of the company. Doc Hortez asked me what had happened so I related all that had transpired. Only Damos knew for sure if he had seen anything. Who were we to question a man who had been in combat for almost thirteen months? The VC-NVA would know we were still in the area and we could expect almost anything this night.

As it turned out nothing materialized. The only contact we had was from a sporadic sniper now and then. He created just enough fear to keep us awake and alert the rest of the night and early morning.

The morning of July 30th dawned bright, muggy, hot, and, as usual, extremely stifling. I had managed to reach my twentieth birthday in the 'Nam. I only hoped I would be around to celebrate number twenty-one!

☆ ☆ ☆ The Waterhole Incident ☆ ☆ ☆
(July 30-August 11, 1967)

We moved out of our blocking position that morning heading for an area known as the Rockpile to run a series of patrols and ambushes. We set up in a perimeter and dug in where we would stay for several days. Doc Hortez and I were taking turns going out on patrols and ambushes that were obtaining negative results and with no contact with the enemy.

Where were they hiding? They were observing us, as the seasoned veterans knew, from their months of experience. Watching and waiting for that one moment when we were more vulnerable than usual.

Word came down from I Corps Intelligence that the VC were using a waterhole some 500 meters from our new perimeter to fill their canteens at night. Where I Corps ever received their information was beyond me. But, with this new bit of information in mind, Lieutenant Adams sent a squad out on an ambush that night. And, as usual, it was my turn to go. The new guy got all the breaks!

At dusk we set out for the waterhole leaving all our clinky-type gear behind so as not to attract attention to ourselves. Corporal Baney, a short-timer in the bush, but a relatively new corporal, had us set up thirty or forty meters off to the side of the waterhole right out in the open with both flanks exposed. He had us covering the waterhole alright, but we were exposed to enemy fire on all sides.

It was pitch black out by the time we were all set in and no one had bothered to scout the area for good cover, concealment, or paths for an escape route if we needed one in a hurry. We were set up on line, including the gun team, facing the waterhole. No rear security! Baney placed me on the right end of the ambush line next to a rifleman and the M-79 grenadier. At this time, McIntyre was a rifleman and Private First Class Loris, the M-79 man, a short-timer due to rotate home soon.

Some hours later we heard noises from our left flank. The VC were coming down a trail right at one of our many exposed areas. We all had to turn to our left and get out of each other's line of fire which cost us precious seconds in response time. They caught us by surprise and opened up with carbines and automatic weapons fire. Lorie immediately caught a round in the belly area but refused medical treatment by me. He just kept firing that grenade launcher like a shotgun. Round after round.

Then, the RTO, Wholper, took some metal shrapnel from either a Chicom grenade or an RPG round. His wounds were superficial and could wait until the firefight was over before I began treatment. I was still worried about Loris's belly wound, as that is one of the worst places to get hit, but he just kept firing like a man possessed. He wouldn't let me work on him for some reason and when the firing ceased we got out of there and high-tailed it back to our perimeter.

Back inside the perimeter Doc Hortez checked Loris's belly wound and called for a medevac chopper. I administered to Wholper's wounds and wrote out a medevac tag as he would need those pieces of jagged metal excised and that was a job for the surgeons back at the Battalion Aid Station.

The medevac chopper came in to a secure LZ and Loris and Wholper went on board with Loris lying on a poncho and Wholper as an ambulatory walking-wounded. Chico explained to me later that he and Loris were really close friends and that was probably why he wouldn't let me treat his wound. It didn't make any sense to me then, nor does it to this day. There was no telling how much damage had been done to his soft organs in the belly area by the enemy bullet.

The next morning, at first light, the entire platoon went down to the waterhole where the brief but intense firefight had been and found no signs of enemy bodies, blood trails, or discarded gear. It was as if the skirmish had never taken place at all although we had two WIAs to prove it had.

☆ ☆ ☆ Operation Lancaster ☆ ☆ ☆
(January 26, 1968)

Lieutenant Holly informed us at a meeting that we were to embark on yet another operation called Operation Lancaster. We were to seek out and destroy the enemy, where he was, sweeping the Demilitarized Zone as far as Con Thien. This area had been our stomping grounds for so long the NVA probably knew us on sight and on a first name basis!

While the Squad Leaders informed their men, I told Doc Maleck about the upcoming operation. It was to begin at 0900 as a Lima

Company endeavor, but instead of the three platoons together, each would have their own special sectors and coordinates to cover and search. One platoon would go south, one west, and the other east. We were to head south moving towards Con Thien about five miles away.

COMFORTING A GRIEVING SOLDIER

At about 0900 we were ready to move out but word came down from the CP to hold and wait. We were already in a staggered column on the side of a hill ready to go when the word was passed down the length of the column. By 1100 we were still waiting and were saturated with sweat when word finally came down the column to move out. Operation Lancaster was finally under way!

Proceeding south we patrolled three or four hours without finding the enemy or any signs of them. This patrol had all the makings of one of those "walk-in-the-park" type of operations.

The afternoon wore on, without any contact with the enemy. We were about 150 meters from A-3, a defensive perimeter manned by Mike Company. They were on a hill and we could look up and see them manning their positions as others went about their routine chores of the day. Likewise, they could look down from their hill and observe us on our sweeping patrol. We were just about "home free" and back to our own area.

We were in a sweeping-type line formation moving through the knee-high undergrowth when Corporal Carruthers spotted a medium-sized cardboard box in front of us. With Lieutenant Holly's permission he looped some rope around the box and backed away with the slack end to get some distance between himself and the box. I told him not to fuck with it as it could be booby-trapped. This was his way of finding out, I guess.

The entire platoon got down as Carruthers tugged on the rope. Nothing happened. It had just been a discarded empty box. Preparing to move out we heard the familiar sound of a mortar round being fired off in the distance on a far hill to our left. We all hit the deck as several rounds came our way but fell short. Apparently, the NVA had been observing us and decided to let us have some rounds just to let us know they were in the vicinity.

On the ground, seeking cover next to Sergeant Allen, I told him how helpless I felt during this kind of attack because all you could do was cover your ass and hope for the best: either a complete miss or a dud round.

The mortar attack lifted as quickly as it had begun and we got up to check with the rest of the men. Luckily, no one had been hit as the rounds fell short for a change. Usually, the enemy mortar crews were quite accurate.

Continuing our sweep, on line, we made our way towards the perimeter of Mike Company. Minutes later Lieutenant Holly received a radio message of, "Friendlies in the area." As the word was being passed up and down the line I spotted two figures in the knee-high undergrowth some fifteen to twenty meters directly in front of me. Thinking of the radio message I turned my head to the left, towards Holly, and said, "Hey, Lieutenant," but by then it was too late. I turned my head to the front and stared at two NVA soldiers. One had an AK-47 mounted on a bipod and pointed right at me. Realizing they were far from friendly I swung my M-16 in front of me but once again it was too late. By thinking about the friendlies it had cost me several precious seconds of decision making. Before I could even squeeze off a burst on automatic I felt my rifle fly from my hands and a searing, burning sensation in my right hand and forearm. The force and closeness of those first rounds spun me around ninety degrees to my left. As I was going down my helmet left my head and I had a painful stinging sensation on the back of my head.

On the ground, with weapons firing all around me, my hand instinctively went to cover the wound to the back of my head. It felt as though my fingers went way into my skull where the bullet wound was located. Thinking I was about to die I closed my eyes and saw brilliant flashing colors. No reliving any fond or past memories. Just beautiful colors. Realizing I was still conscious I opened my eyes only to be hit in the forearm with shrapnel from either a Chicom grenade or mortar round. The blast lifted me off the ground and threw me back down again. The concussion was tremendous.

By this time the entire platoon was moving and began throwing all the firepower they could muster towards the enemy. Private First Class "Rock" Realin was the first to reach me and, making sure I was still alive, yelled for Doc Maleck (not his real name). As I had been the first man hit I asked Realin if anyone else had been wounded. So far, I was the only casualty.

Once Doc Maleck arrived I should have been relieved but I wasn't. He looked scared and totally inept. He wrapped a field dressing around my right hand and forearm, but when he came to my head wound he didn't know how to go about treating it, so I had to tell him what to do. Sergeant Allen came over and—I'll never forget this as long as I live—said to Maleck, "If anything happens to him, (me), I'll shoot your dumb ass!" Maleck just stared at Allen in total disbelief. I thought he was going to cry. The "Sarge" was outstanding. That's the kind of Marine he was and you can tell what type of medical corpsman Maleck represented.

I told Maleck to place some sterile four-by-four gauze pads on my head wound. He then wrapped them securely with an ace bandage around my forehead and under my chin to hold them in place. At this point Lieutenant Corporal Pecora came over to me and asked if I wanted him to say a prayer for me. (He had been the Second Platoon CP radioman for some time but was now the chaplain's assistant.) We were good friends and I said "yes" to his offer of a prayer.

My pain wasn't too bad. Just a burning and throbbing of my hand and head so maybe a prayer was in order. I was still alive and that was worth something.

The firing had almost ceased by now and Doc Maleck was finishing wrapping my wounds and tagging me when four of our men came over with a poncho. They carried me to the LZ where the medevac chopper would land. While lying in the poncho, waiting for the chopper, two other men from the platoon were also carried over to the LZ. Corporal Dougherty, of the machine gun squad, had been wounded in the knee and Private First Class Bowser had been hit in his size twelve foot.

As we were placed on board the chopper I managed to sit up and wave to no one in particular. I certainly had mixed emotions right then. I did not want to leave my men, especially in the incapable hands of Doc Maleck. But I was glad to be out of the threat of constant danger which haunts every man or woman serving in a combat zone. Never knowing if that next step will be your last. Afraid of not seeing that trip-wire strung along the ground near your ankle. The thought of coming back out into the field again was the farthest thing from my mind at the time.

We were flown to Camp Carroll which was the headquarters for the Third Battalion, Fourth Marines and the Battalion Aid Station there for triage and treatment. It was ironic because this was the same area I had reported to just seven months earlier upon my arrival in the 'Nam. What goes around, comes around, I guess.

Exiting the chopper we were assisted to the large BAS where we shed all our combat gear. Sitting on a bench to await treatment a doctor saw me and said to one of the corpsmen, "Get that man on a table!" Being a head-wound case the corpsman should have known enough to have me lie down but they were busy with other casualties much worse than me. We certainly had not been the only unit to get hit that day.

Once on the examining table I felt the urge to urinate like crazy! Receiving a urinal from a corpsman I tried to go but couldn't. One medic then began unwrapping the dressings from my hand and forearm while the other removed the bandages from my head wound. Two physicians came over to me and, after placing their fingers in and on my head wound, one said to the other, "I can feel the swelling. The bullet is still in there. Let's get this man to X-ray."

The results brought a sigh of relief to me, that's for sure, as I had suffered a badly mangled fifth digit on the right hand, small fragments of metal in my right forearm, which are still there to this day, and a laceration to my posterior scalp. So the bullet was not in there after all! Thank the Lord!

WITH THE 3/27

by Robert Simonsen

There is an old Marine Corps saying that "every Marine is a basic rifleman." This was never proven more true than in February, 1968. The Marine Corps was ordered to send an entire infantry regiment to offset the Tet offensive in Vietnam. They responded with the Twenty-seventh Marines, a Fifth Marine Division unit that had last fought on Iwo Jima during World War II. The Twenty-seventh, however, was vastly understrengthed. It was basically a training and Vietnam replacement unit, made up of new Marines just out of boot camp and seasoned veterans waiting to get out of the Corps. Nearly 800 were non-deployable, which meant they needed an additional 950 Marines to bring it up to full strength. The Third Battalion (3/27), being the last battalion to form up, had great difficulty in finding enough infantry-related Marines at Camp Pendleton, California. They were forced to take every available Marine on the base to fill their ranks. Nearly half of the Marines were not infantry trained except for the initial training they received after joining the Corps. They became a bastard battalion—jokingly referred to as a "cooks, baker, and candlestick maker" unit!

I was a construction surveyor with the Thirteenth Engineers when I was transferred to 3/27, where I was immediately made a fire-team leader. My squad had a cook, a truck driver, a mechanic, a draftsman, and other non-infantry Marines. We formed up in just two days and flew, as a battalion, to Vietnam on the third day. The next day we were running combat patrols. We learned fast, sometimes costly lessons, but we soon became a good fighting unit. We met the NVA head on during Operation Allenbrook in May, 1968, and were awarded the Meritorious Unit Citation for helping to stop the NVA from attacking the city of Danang.

The rifle training that Marines receive every year, and the initial combat training we get after boot camp, allowed our mixed bunch of Marines to perform their task admirably. During Operation

Allenbrook alone, we received one Medal of Honor, two Navy Crosses, fourteen Silver Stars, and numerous Bronze Stars. Our Medal of Honor winner, Robert Burke, was an auto mechanic when he was transferred to 3/27. We proved that every Marine can quickly adapt to any situation and can perform as a combat Marine.

THE AK-47

In 1943, Red Army leadership saw the effects the new relatively light, easily produced, German MP44 was taking on their men. They commissioned the Kalashnikov works to produce a similar or superior weapon for their own troops. The gas-operated AK-47 was the result. The original model featured a receiver machined from a block of solid steel with an interior chrome-plated barrel. This was a rugged weapon with a minimum number of moving parts. It could stand field conditions that would compromise other weapons.

The war ended before the AK-47 could reach the hands of infantry units, but by the early 1950's, it was the standard weapon of Soviet forces. And soon every satellite and client state either was supplied or were manufacturing them.

It was the standard Viet Cong weapon during the Vietnam War. Though not without its faults, particularly accuracy over 300 meters, it was a superior weapon to the early M-16s that American forces were issued.

AK-47s are still widely in use today.

TET OFFENSIVE IN THE MEKONG DELTA

by Ronald J. Diver

I shot the first guy square in the face, snapping his head back, throwing him to the ground on his back where he flopped like a chicken just beheaded by Mom back on the Wisconsin farm. Because I'd fired my M-16 from the hip without having time to draw a bead, I'd shot high when I'd realized that a whole damn squad of VC had just run right smack into me. The second man in the squad wasn't very lucky because I had time to aim at him and the round struck him low in the chest, dropping him in the dust of the old road. The third man was swift on his feet and dove into the deep ditch that bordered the road, preparing to fire at me, his buddies along side of him. I was in deep shit and knew it! It was the fourth day of the Tet Offensive, which had kicked off at exactly 0300 on the 31st of January 1968.

I heard the jeep engine roar into life behind me and I turned, sprinting for the vehicle as if my life depended on it, which it did. Doc Davis (not his real name), my esteemed boss, a surgeon, and a captain in the U.S. Air Force, looked like he was getting very ready to swiftly depart the area and I knew that if he did, I was a dead man. I was ready to pull down on him with my M-16 if he made that move to leave me, and I probably would have if he hadn't hesitated, giving me time to damn near herniate myself getting into the right seat on the old jeep.

When the Viet Cong struck us on the morning of January 31st, we were waiting patiently for them to show their hand. We being fifty American advisors, a large component of the ARVN (Army of the Republic of Vietnam), and numerous militia, the Regional Forces/Popular Forces (RF/PF). We, hereafter called the good guys, outnumbered the communists by two to one, and they were attacking our fortified positions, which is not considered healthy in anyone's book. We got overrun once and the firefights were pretty hairy, but, as soon as it got light and we got some A1Es to drop some ordinance containing napalm, the VC quickly lost their appetite for battle and withdrew. By the third day, there was no more enthusiasm in their half-hearted attacks, but we had decided that it might be a good idea to move and bury some of their dead that were stacked up around the compounds. Bulldozer time! The local soccer field became a mass grave when we dug a huge hole and filled it quickly so we could breath again. I don't know what the history books will say, but, as a participant, I'd say the bad guys lost about 500 of their finest while we lost 3 Americans, about 50 ARVN, and about 125 RF/PF troops. Not a good trade for Charlie! When the call came again from Hanoi in May, 1968, to attack our positions, all they could field was old men and some kids and it didn't last long.

THE END OF THE VIET CONG AT TET

The Lunar New Year is Vietnam is called Tet. In 1967 the Viet Cong throughout the war-torn nation launched a massive offensive. At its height, the American Embassy in Saigon was seized by guerillas. It was re-taken by U.S. Marines with heavy casualties on both sides. The fighting in and around the city of Hue was particularly intense.

Beyond the military targets, a major political offensive was also being waged. This one was not on the streets of Vietnamese cities but in the perception of American voters. More and more, American popular support for the war and the Johnson Administration waned.

While the Tet Offensive failed to achieve any military goals, during the two months it was waged it did raise serious questions about the conduct of the war and the way it was being waged.

By the time the smoke cleared and the last ground taken by the Viet Cong reclaimed by American and ARVN troops, it was evident that the war had entered a new phase. The Viet Cong had taken so many casualties that they effectively ceased to exist. It would take years to redevelop the cadre and infrastructure expended with no gain. Counting the Japanese occupation, the French-Indo Chinese War, and the American involvement, Vietnam had been at war for close to thirty continuous years. They were running out of time to keep fighting. Even as their leadership proclaimed they would fight on, the responsibility for conducting the war passed completely to the People's Republic of Vietnam in the north.

By spring, the remnants of the Viet Cong were relegated to support roles. The North Vietnamese Army had moved into position and became the major opponent of American and ARVN forces.

PATROL

Stephen Maxwell

One day while on twelve-hour patrol in downtown Saigon, a Vietnamese kid, about twelve to fourteen years old walked by the back of our gun jeep. He said something and threw an object in the back and ran off. I yelled "grenade" and both my driver and I jumped out. The jeep kept going towards the open market. We yelled for people to get down but nothing happened. We went back to the jeep and found an orange had been thrown. What next?

PFC STEPHEN MAXWELL
Jump School, 1964

LRRPS IN VIETNAM

Long Range Reconnaissance Patrols were the eyes and ears on the American presence in Vietnam. These were small, highly professional elite units that would be inserted into enemy-held territory. Their missions were usually observation, artillery spotting, and interdiction.

Very similar missions were also carried out by Recon Marines. Occasionally Navy SEAL team members took part in LRRP missions when their objectives overlapped.

Towards the end of the war their mission (and their name changed). Now called LRP, they were called on to take more active measures, including initiating contact to lure NVA regulars into the sights of helicopter gun-ships and artillery.

Patrol size varied, but most were well under ten men led by a NCO. While the average age on American soldiers in Vietnam was 19, LRRPs tended to be in their early 20's.

Ranger training was only the beginning of the qualifications a LRRP team member needed to survive the tension and constant danger of field missions. Indeed, after becoming a "Tab" Ranger (graduating from Ranger school in the United States), a LRRP candidate would be re-trained by veterans in Vietnam. The last part of the training program was an actual mission into NVA-held territory.

THE TOWER MAN
by Philip White

I was getting some work done on my car that was covered by an extended warranty. It was taking forever. The young man trying to figure out the forms was being supervised by an older guy wearing an old black beret. He saw my growing frustration and said, "Relax, it's too dark out now to play golf."

I said jokingly, "I'm not a golfer. I'm a sniper."

"No, you're not. I am," he countered. There was something in the way he said it that made me prompt for more information.

"How many tours did you do?" I asked.

"Three. Mostly in 'Nam. I was in SEAL Team Two," which completely captured my attention. "I was the tower man. I was the best shot in the team. My job was to find high ground and lay down cover or suppressing fire. And I was the McGyver. I could fix anything. That's why I'm fixing cars now."

He was a big man. Over six feet tall with a build that showed the years, but also showed that he was once much stronger. "I could hump the big guns. So I got the job of humping the big guns."

He told of training, missions to countries that raised my eyebrows, and lots of SEAL missions in 'Nam and stateside. He went on to talk about ongoing missions to test Naval base security. Swimming into a base and kidnapping the commander, hog-tying SP's, and deviltry like that.

I told him that Richard Marcinko mentioned that in his book *Rogue Warrior*. He replied, "All the Teams do that. It's good training and it improves base security. Pissing off officers is fun too." (No base commander ever wants a SEAL Team to make a surprise visit). "I never met Marcinko. But he was the real thing when he was in the Teams. People give him grief because he's so successful. That's just TFB.

"I was in the Teams early. Back then we were still pretty much Underwater Demolition Team oriented. By the time Marcinko and

Team Six came along, the focus changed."

He pulled a few papers from his wallet. One was the list of citations he won along with a brief summary of his naval service. It was very impressive. Yet while he was very proud his accomplishments, I never for a moment heard a tone of bravado or bragging. He was good. And he was talking because he sensed I was interested. And it helped pass the time. During our conversation I noticed that he seemed to be turning to the right whenever I asked him anything.

"How much hearing loss do you have?" I asked.

"Enough to separate me from the service." But he changed the subject quickly. "I meant it when I said I'm a good shot." He showed me a document listing the weapons he's licensed to own and yet another of trophies, awards, and competitions he either won or placed high in. They included Camp Perry.

Now, he hunts deer with a pistol. I asked him to save some venison for me. That means I'll have to go back and talk some more with him.

HOMECOMING
by Sean Spruck

D ad arrived in Vietnam on February 10, 1970, and was sent to
Fire Support Base Charlie 1 up by the DMZ. On February
13th it was overrun by the NVA. He spent five months in the bush
leading Long Range Reconnaissance Patrols (LRRPs). He rarely
took a day off from leading teams out for four to six days. Then his
Commander broke the LRRP teams up and gave my dad a job of
flying in the back seat of an O-1 Birddog observation plane. Daily,
sometimes as many as four times a day, he and his pilot would take
off and go looking "down low" for the enemy. If they saw anything
he would call arty (artillery) or an air strike to hit the target. It was-
n't much safer because Dad and his pilots were shot down three
different times. Each time (thank God) they walked away, got
another airplane (sometimes the same day), and flew again. On
December 11th, no one was flying due to bad weather. When Dad
called in the nightly report to Twenty-fourth Corps Headquarters he
was told to report to the battalion formation the next morning at
Gia Le, Phu Bai. Dad stood in back of the morning formation and
was surprised to hear his name called. When he reported to the
major in charge, Dad learned he was there to receive medals awarded for his actions his third day in-country and for his actions in
saving one of his pilot's lives when they were shot down.

Later at the club the major asked Dad why he wasn't happy. Dad
told him he was not looking forward to missing his first Christmas
and his first anniversary with his wife. Then the major reached in his
pocket and pulled my dad's DEROS (Date Estimated Return from
Overseas) papers out and told Dad he was going home on
December 24th. Dad couldn't have been happier. He reported back
to the 220th RAC late in the afternoon and went to schedule the
board for the next day's missions. The major from the 220th was
there and saw Dad schedule himself for a very difficult mission with
a new pilot deep inside the A Shau Valley. The major erased my dad's

name and told him he knew he was "short," and added he had flown more missions, took the toughest missions, trained more new pilots, and kept the air observer crew in line and deserved a break.

Dad flew to Camh Ranh Bay on December 19th. On December 23rd he learned he was being "bumped" to December 25th. Then someone told him about the International Date Line. If he left on December 25th and flew all day and night when he got home it would still be December 25th. Dad left Vietnam at 6:06 A.M. on December 25, 1970. When he landed at McChord Air Force Base it was 5:45 A.M. Christmas morning. There were hundreds of volunteers to hem pants and dress greens, process leave papers and pay. Dad flew out of Seattle/Tacoma International Airport at 9:00 A.M. on December 25th and landed at LaGuardia Airport at 6:30 P.M. There he found out that the small commuter airline which was to get him to his hometown by 10:00 P.M. was on strike. He took a taxi to Port Authority in New York City where at 10:30 P.M. Christmas night he caught a bus for home. Eleven hours later it pulled into Corning, New York, my dad and mom's hometown. They had had six inches of snow the night before and in the morning when the bus arrived it was bright and sunny.

Dad took a taxi to Caton where Mom had moved back in with her mother and father on their country farm. The taxi struggled to get up the slick road to the farm. My dad had it stop before the homestead and walked the last quarter mile. When he dropped his duffel bag on the porch and walked in, all he saw was his father-in-law, mother-in-law, and Mom's sisters and brothers. Mom's youngest sister ran upstairs hollering for Mom to come down, "your husband is home!" My mom got angry at her sister saying he would have called to let her know he was on his way home. Her sister had to lead her down the stairs to the kitchen where Dad waited. Through her tears of happiness my mom told me she hugged Dad and never wanted to let him go. "Why didn't you call?" she kept asking.

Almost thirty-one years have gone by and my dad and mom are still together. Together they raised three children into successful adults.

SPITSHINE

by James L. Swanson

S pitshining leather is a ritual that for more than two centuries was done only by Marines. American Marines learned it from British Marines, who for some reason, gave it up years ago. It's a simple procedure that produces incredible results.

After removing the lid from your can of Kiwi, you fill the lid with water. You wrap your first or second finger in an old T-shirt, dip it in the water, then in the polish. Then you make small circles on the leather. If you have too much polish, thin it with a little water. If you have too much water, thicken it with a little polish. Make small circles on the leather. Never rub, never use a brush, never use a shoe cloth.

After a while, patience will reward you. You'll begin to see your face. Not features, yet, but an outline. Then in a few more minutes, the features will be discernible. Now, with just a little more patience, a little more polish and water, you'll see pinpoints of light dance upon the leather. You've learned how to spitshine. Proudly, you put your shoes away, ready for Saturday morning's inspection.

Today it's different. Marines no longer spitshine their shoes. I learned this piece of gut-wrenching news while boarding a bus [one] day in San Diego from a gunnery sergeant, a senior drill instructor and one of our group leaders. He stood by the door of the bus helping the ladies board, and as I was about to board, proud of the fact that I still spitshine my shoes, I stuck my foot out and placed it next to his.

"What d'ya think?" I asked.

He glanced down at our shoes, side by side on the curbing. Then he shook his head. "Not even close," he said. "Nowadays, we cheat."

I looked down at his ultra shiny, perfect, unblemished patent-leather shoes and almost had a heart attack. The Army, Air Force, the Coast Guard, even the Navy I could understand—but Marines? I must have looked like I was about to faint. The DI reached over and steadied me.

"Sorry, Sir," he said. "We haven't spitshined our shoes for a number of years now. We're issued these instead." He turned his foot so I could see the whole length of his shoe. It was a nice looking shoe—it even looked like a Marine shoe—black, clean, shiny. But it wasn't spitshined. It was made of patent leather and it sort of glowed all over. But it was no spitshine.

I believe today's Marines have lost something important, something personal that cannot be replaced by ten pairs of patent-leather shoes. The small amount of time saved can never replace the values we learned by spitshining our shoes and our leather. Spitshining your leather allows time for reflection, teaches patience, and perhaps, gives us a small amount of humility. I can't help but feel the Corps has lost something of value.